Rev. William J. Bausch

FOREWORD BY MSGR. JOSEPH M. CHAMPLIN

TAKE

HEART,

FATHER

A Hope-Filled Vision for
TODAY'S PRIEST

TWENTY-THIRD PUBLICATIONS
Mystic, Connecticut

Other Books by the Author

Storytelling: Imagination and Faith
Pilgrim Church
A New Look at the Sacraments
The Christian Parish
Ministry: Traditions, Tensions, Transitions

Twenty-Third Publications
P.O. Box 180
Mystic, CT 06355
(203) 536-2611

ISBN 0-89622-309-4
Library of Congress Catalog Card Number 86-50893
Edited by Walter Nott
Interior design by John van Bemmel

Pro fratribus

and a few *sororibus*

Foreword

A GROUP OF CATHOLIC CLERGY FROM THE NORTHWEST GATHERED at a Minnesota retreat center several months ago to discuss the future of priestly ministry in the United States. Because of the statistical surveys projecting an imminent shortage of priests so frequently published today and the radical shifts in pastoral activities so often experienced by priests themselves, these leaders wanted to pursue the following kind of crucial issues and questions: What will the priesthood be like in the year 2000? How can priestless parishes function? Is the priest still important?

I was asked to offer some input to this gathering and heard, via the clerical grapevine, that Father Bill Bausch had recently delivered a fine major address on the very topic. In a typically generous response to my request for some information about his presentation, the New Jersey pastor sent me a cassette of that lecture. His remarks are informative, visionary, and helpful.

Much of that talk and much more will be found in this book.

On many levels the shepherd of St. Mary's Parish, "A Christian Community in the Roman Catholic Tradition," at Colts Neck, New Jersey, offers great modeling for today's priests. Moreover, his writing, both in several practical pastoral books and now with *Take Heart, Father: A Hope-Filled Vision for Today's Priest,* reflect, as we might expect, those role model activities.

Father Bausch reads.

Our contemporary clergy, especially those in pastoral or parish ministry, find it difficult to locate space for serious reading, organized study, or even available lectures. There are such demands upon time and energy that discovering opportunities for updating or at least justifying the hours or days for them is an ongoing struggle.

Bill Bausch has consistently done this. His older, and recently revised, expanded, and updated *A New Look at the Sacraments* grew out of an adult education lecture series for parishioners at St. Mary's. However, to give those talks meant hours of preparation by a concerned pastor seeking to translate the best of current thinking into understandable terms for his people.

Take Heart, Father likewise reveals a priest who continues assiduously to follow both secular and religious writers and speakers. You will note here references to *Megatrends* and *Search for Excellence* as well as excerpts from the documents of the Second Vatican Council and the Revised Code of Canon Law.

Father Bausch responds.

Bill Bausch is constantly listening to people, discerning their needs, and conceiving creative ways of responding to those situations.

I have cited many times in lectures across this country his workable ideas sketched in *The Christian Parish* and *Ministry: Traditions, Tensions, Transitions* for example, I judge as eminently practical the "one-to-one ministry" at St. Mary's by which people who have suffered through certain challenges or burdens in their lives, from adoption to terminal illness, are willing to share with others in a confidential setting their own experiences. A list of 20 problems or issues followed by the name and phone number of the "experienced" person is published in the parish's impressive annual book of activities.

Take Heart, Father provides additional illustrations of the latest pastoral "inventions" at Colts Neck which respond to parishioners' various needs.

Father Bausch organizes.

These numerous down-to-earth developments could not materialize without a leader's proven ability to harness the efforts of many people in an organized, systematic manner. Chapter VIII, "Principles of Collaboration," tells us how Father Bausch has done this and also outlines some useful tips on how they can follow his example.

Bill Bausch begins this book by relating to the pain of today's priests "whose fractured identity is in sore need of healing, affirmation, and clarity." The pages of *Take Heart, Father* supply a good measure of that necessary healing, affirmation, and clarity. The text ends with the New Jersey pastor indicating that the contemporary priest's new role of a shared and collaborative ministry, "once you get on to it, is positively joyous." This kind of ministering is different from the past, more time-consuming and less certainly defined, but it is essential, liberating, and full of satisfaction

I hope many priests will read Father Bausch's latest book, gain through it a clearer vision of their critical function in the contemporary church, and taste the kind of joy that a harmonizing style of leadership can give them.

Rev. Joseph M. Champlin
Vicar for Parish Life and Worship
Syracuse, New York

Contents

Introduction

*John McLoughlin that lived out on the Point Road
had this hound. There was never the beating of
her. She pupped in a teapot.*

*One time she was carrying the pups and a rabbit
ran out and she made after it and ripped the belly
out of herself on this ditch, on a wire or
something; and the pups, the greyhound pups,
spilled out of her. And one of them jumped up
like hell and ran after the rabbit and stuck right
with it until he caught and killed it.*

*And when the greyhound died, John McLoughlin
had her skinned and he put a back in a waistcoat
with her skin. And one day he was out over the
water hunting and this rabbit shot out; and begod
he said, the back of the waistcoat on him
barked!*[1]

NOW, THAT'S A TALL STORY. BUT I LIKE IT NOT ONLY BECAUSE IT IS
funny but because it strikes a note I would like this book to
have, a note of persistent hope, or, if you will, hopeful per-
sistence. I think we need to hear this, we priests, because
clerical times are hard and morale seems low. I think we need
to sit back and search out the light in these dark times. But

1

I also think there *is* light to be found, new ways of priesting and, in general, an exciting breakthrough awaiting us.

So this book is dedicated to re-visioning who and what we are and suggesting hope for the future. It ranges from the sometimes theoretical to the more-often practical. I hardly expect that everyone will agree with either the theory or the practice, but I would wish that everyone would get something, however small, from it. This book, in fact, completes a trilogy starting with *The Christian Parish* (1980) and *Ministry: Traditions, Tensions, and Transitions in Ministry* (1982).[2] There is some inevitable overlap, very insignificant (in Chapter VIII), but this is a whole new book going beyond the parish and ministry to the priest himself whose fractured identity is in sore need of healing, affirmation, and clarity. And, although the book is addressed to priests, I would dearly hope that all God's people would read it because I sincerely believe that the people, increasingly our collaborators, should get insight into where we're coming from and journey with us to where we are (communally) going.

At the beginning and end of each chapter, you will notice, there are (mostly clerical) stories and jokes. Life can be grim enough to make us take ourselves too seriously. A little self-inflicted laughter can go a long way to easing our confusion and nudging us along on a journey that for two thousand years has, for the most part, been enhanced and brightened by the particular and singular charisms of our confreres.

Three final items. First, I have no illusions about any originality in this book beyond my own filtering and perceptions and biases. My modest aim has been to draw together from many scattered sources what so many have already been saying. There are many prophetic voices and I am indebted to them. Second, you will notice that throughout I refer mostly to pastors. This is not to slight priest associates but only to recognize that they have a different status in some ways and that, of course, eventually, they will be pastors, so they are in reality included in these remarks. Third, I want to thank

Monsignor Joseph Champlin who took time from a busy schedule to read the manuscript and make valuable suggestions. I am especially grateful for those suggestions which moved me a bit closer to the kindness and sensitivity he possesses by nature and grace.

A Prologue of Clever Things

To: Jesus, Son of Joseph
   Woodcrafter Carpenter Shop
   Nazareth 25922

From: Jordan Management Consultants
   Jerusalem 26544

Dear Sir:

Thank you for submitting the resumés of the twelve men you have picked for management positions in your new organization. All of them have now taken our battery of tests; we have not only run the results through our computer, but also arranged personal interviews for each of them with our psychologists and vocational aptitude consultant. The profiles of all tests are included, and you will want to study each of them carefully.

As part of our service and for your guidance, we make some general comments, much as an auditor will include some general statements. This is given as a result of staff consultation and comes without any additional fees.

It is the staff opinion that most of your nominees are lacking in background, education and vocational aptitude for the type of enterprise you are undertaking. They do not have the team concept. We would recommend that you continue your search for persons of experience in managerial ability and proven capability.

Simon Peter is emotionally unstable and given to fits of

4

temper. Andrew has absolutely no qualities of leadership. The two brothers, James and John, the sons of Zebedee, place personal interest above company loyalty. Thomas demonstrates a questioning attitude that would tend to undermine morale. We feel that it is our duty to tell you that Matthew has been black-listed by the Greater Jerusalem Better Business Bureau. James, son of Alpheus, and Thaddaeus definitely have radical leanings, and they both registered a high score on the manic-depressive scale.

One of the candidates, however, shows great potential. He is a man of ability and resourcefulness, meets people well, has a keen business mind, and has contacts in high places. He is highly motivated, ambitious and responsible. We recommend Judas Iscariot as your controller and right-hand man. All other profiles are self-explanatory.

We wish you every success in your new venture.

Sincerely yours,

Jordan Management Counsultants

(from St. Andrew's Episcopal Church newsletter, Meeteetse, Wyoming)

The priest's shortcomings simply cannot be concealed. On the contrary, even the most trivial soon gets known...For as long as the priest's life is well regulated in every particular point, the intrigues cannot hurt him. But if he should overlook some small detail, as is likely for a human being on his journey across the devious ocean of life, all the rest of his good deeds are of no avail to enable him to escape the words of his accusers. That small offense casts a shadow over all the rest of his life. Everyone wants to judge the priest, not as one clothed in flesh, not as one possessing a human nature, but as an angel, exempt from the frailty of others.

(From "the more things change," etc., department; written 1500 years ago by St. John Chrysostom.)

"More misery, Hester!—only the more misery!" answered the clergyman, with a bitter smile. "As concerns the good which I may appear to do, I have no faith in it. It must needs be a delusion. What can a ruined soul, like mine, effect towards the redemption of other souls?—or a polluted soul toward their purification? And as for the people's reverence, would that it were turned to scorn and hatred! Canst thou deem it, Hester, a consolation, that I must stand up in my pulpit, and meet so many eyes turned upward to my face, as if the light of Heaven were beaming from it!—must see my flock hungry for the truth, and listening to my words as if a tongue of Pentecost were speaking!—and then look inward and discern the black reality of what they idolize? I have laughed, in bitterness and agony of heart, at the contrast between what I seem and what I am!

(The Reverend Dimsdale, in a bad moment, from Nathaniel Hawthorne's The Scarlet Letter.)

"Pooh!" cried Piglet, and now it was *his* turn to be the admiring one. "You've saved us!"
"Have I?" said Pooh, not feeling quite sure.

(Theologian without portfolio, A.A. Milne.)

Every year at the seminary the composite senior class picture is hung in the seminary corridor. A Bible verse that best identifies the class accompanies the photograph. One professor, asked what verse might be appropriate for this particular class, replied, "John 11:35." Students scurried to find the words he had chosen: "Jesus wept."

I

Megatrends

JOHN NAISBITT HAS POPULARIZED THE TERM *MEGATREND* TO INDICATE profound long-range changes, perceptions, and ways of life in our society. We have only to test our own history in the last few centuries to see how such megatrends, once so novel, have become commonplace today. The Industrial Revolution, for example, brought about massive migrations from farms to factories, resulting in new ways of thinking about life and living. Politics since the eighteenth century has moved us from castles to congresses and our taken-for-granted democratic assumptions. Our own recent civil rights movements have literally and figuratively moved us from the back to the front of the bus. These are long-range changes influencing our habits of thinking and perceiving, moving us from the old patterns based on ancient tradition and myths to those of modern humanism and science.

In the Catholic church we are undergoing the same kind

7

of ecclesiastical megatrends which are affecting and will affect our traditional Catholic ways of ministry, service, and organization. Professor Richard Schoenherr, Associate Professor of sociology at the University of Wisconsin-Madison has made a close statistical study of the church for the past twenty years, especially in regard to the waxing and waning of clerical numbers and the profound implications such declining numbers have for us all.[1] As a result of his studies he sees ten counter-punctual megatrends, five concerning decline and five concerning growth, which are in absolute tension with one another and buck many centuries of tradition. It will be helpful in this chapter to use his categories as discussion points of who we are and where we are going as priests. We'll list them in a series of five sets of opposing forces.

The First Tension: The decline in the number of priests (and religious) vs. the growth of the number of nonordained ministers or lay leaders. From 1966 to 1985 Professor Schoenherr has verified what we already know from the papers and popular magazines: Ordinations are down, and the future does not look promising. Based on several projections, including those officially issued by the Vatican, there were in 1970 some 37,000 diocesan priests for about 53 million Catholics in the United States. By the year 2000—which is, after all, little more than ten years away—there will be an estimated 13,000 to 15,000 diocesan priests in the United States for about 65 to 75 million Catholics. A moderate upswing is predicted around 1990 (based on a backward look at history in a similar crisis in France), but the overall decline is there. In short, based on the ratios of men entering the seminary plus those existing priests who are retiring, dying, and resigning, indications are that in the year 2000 there will be 50 percent fewer priests serving 35 percent more Catholics than in the year 1980. Or, if you want to translate all this into more impressionable terms, note that Chicago, the second largest diocese in the U.S. with 2.3 million Catholics, ordained ten priests in 1985. And note that Father Tom Sweester says that, based on current seminary enrollments, only 319 men will be ordained in 1988 for the entire United States.

You can see that when Pope John Paul II wrote to the bishops of the United States, "This decline in numbers is a matter of grave concern to me," he was rightly upset, but I suspect he did not know the full story contained in that phrase above "based on current seminary enrollment." There is a "youth drain," no doubt about it. From 1962 when Vatican II began until 1984, seventy-six seminaries either closed or merged in our country. There are now half as many students preparing for the priesthood as at the start of the Council, and all but one-third of those are members of religious congregations. In the forty-nine Roman Catholic schools that belong to the Association of Theological Schools, there are almost 3000 students engaged in theological studies, but none of them are seeking ordination. According to CARA (Center for Applied Research in the Apostolate) the combined total for all U.S. students for the priesthood declined fron 11,585 in 1984-85 to 10,811 the following year, down 7 percent. The largest drop was in the number of seminarians at the college level, which declined by 12 percent. The number of theology students was down by almost 3 percent and the number of high school seminarians dropped by 4 percent.

When you have all this decline in vocations and/or perseverance, people are always seeking causes. The U.S. Catholic Conference in its survey on men's vocations tried to zero in on a few of these causes. One, they said, is a down trend in participation in Catholic life following Vatican II. They cite the survey showing the percentage of Catholics who felt that religion was important in their lives dropped from 83 percent in 1952 to 56 percent in 1980. Mass attendance has statistically dropped off. With that kind of decline in interest and participation, vocations are not easily fostered. Second, the report maintains that Catholics have become more critical of their priests than in the past, and from 1963 to 1974, the percentage of Catholics who indicated that they would be very pleased to have a son a priest dropped from 66 percent to 55 percent. Third, the old large families, ethnic ties, stability, and stable upbringing have certainly declined—all factors in promoting vocations. Fourth, Catholics have been so assimilated into the American success dream, higher incomes, status, and a varied and fast-lane lifestyle that there is little attraction by comparison for the priesthood. Finally, in today's climate, the issue of celibacy has given many pause. In 1980 a study of 1,400 young men showed that 51 percent of those who have in fact thought of entering the seminary said that the celibacy factor was an issue in not deciding to enter and 33 percent balked at the prospect of a lifelong commitment.

From the person in the street comes this assessment of the problem, namely that the cause of all this decline and disinterest lies in the fact that

> after World War II, vast numbers of Catholic youth began going to colleges and universities on the G.I. Bill of Rights, on scholarships, on the foundations, on state and federal loans and on their improved family finances. On graduation they found professional and managerial positions or established their own businesses, vacated the old urban ghettos...Thus they integrated with their Protestant and Jewish peers into the "mainstream" of modern American society.

> Let's face it. Entrance into seminaries and convents in bygone years may have been religiously motivated, but they were also catalyzed by poverty, inability to get into colleges and universities, strong religious mother figures, weak or deceased father figures, overplayed devotional Catholicism...and a host of archaic attitudes that were swept away in the 1960s.[2]

Well, whatever the causes, the figures of decline speak for themselves.

This youth drain also has another side beyond the statistics of those *not* entering the seminaries: those already ordained but who have resigned. In the immediate decade prior to Vatican II, for example, resignations rose by less than one-tenth of 1 percent. In the immediate decade after Vatican

II, resignations rose by 13 percent and then to 17 percent in 1980. Or, to put it another way, statistics show that by their tenth anniversary of ordination 20 percent of all priests have resigned. By their fifteenth anniversary 15 percent have resigned and by their silver jubilee 42 percent have resigned. In fact, statistics as of 1985 indicate that, if the present trend continues, in three to four years there will be as many resigned priests as active ones, and it is quite likely that even later there will be *more* resigned than active clergy.

Finally, to add to all this distressing news, is the obvious fact that the clergy, like the rest of America, is graying. The evidence is all around us as we see the predominance of gray and balding heads at any clergy gathering. Our mean age is over fifty and is getting meaner each year. In the year 2000 it will be close to seventy! Moreover, we can expect age's predictable by-product: conservatism—and the tension this will bring. As Professor Schoenherr's report observes:

> We can expect an increase of conservatism in the organizational climate of local dioceses as the age structure changes to a predominantly older clergy. . . . It is commonly noted among seminary professors that recent cohorts of seminarians are more conservative socially, politically and theologically than those of the 1960s and early 1970s. . . . As fewer young men are ordained the probability increases that those who are will have well-examined and therefore lasting commitments to the clerical ministry. Since resignations have been more frequent among priests who espouse more liberal Catholic beliefs and values, and the proportion of more conservative priests with stronger commitments to their ministry is likely to increase, we could expect fewer resignations in the future. . . . As one category expands and the other contracts, the clergy in the next couple of decades automatically becomes a more homogeneous group and so less subject to conflict—and therefore less open to innovation—than the clergy of the Second Vatican Council period. Our data and projections lend considerable support to the conclusion that the demo-

graphic transition in progress will result in a smaller, older, more conservative and more homogeneous population of priests.[3]

We can see the practical result of all these ominous figures operating already. When you have lots of personnel, resources, and money you can afford to experiment and be prodigal, but when these items are in short supply you have to be careful how you dole them out. Thus a headline from the March 20, 1985 *New York Times:* "O'Connor intends to shift more priests to parishes." The reference is to the then Archbishop John O'Connor of New York who is quoted in the paper as saying, "The parishes are hurting." He noted that in the past year he has buried 32 priests out of 754 active ones with a median age of 55. O'Connor has replaced his 38 priests in chancery administration (hangover from prodigal times) with lay people, nuns, and deacons and put them into parishes (scarcity times). The diocese of Nashville has decreed that priests may celebrate no more than one Mass a day nor more than two on Sundays. In Madison, Wisconsin, three parishes were reduced to mission status and are served by priests from neighboring parishes. Dioceses in Massachusetts, Connecticut, Rhode Island, New Jersey, and others have reduced the number of weekend Masses in order "to lighten the stress on priests." Sisters are being appointed parish administrators (e.g., Charlotte, North Carolina); offices to train laity for jobs formerly handled only by clergy are being opened all over the country (e.g., Des Moines and Newark); deacons are pastoring more and more parishes; and some dioceses (e.g., Brooklyn) have celebrated No-Priest Day to dramatize the priest shortage. On a larger scale, scarcity is at work in the figures of the 1984 Official Catholic Directory which shows that 983 of the 19,118 parishes in our country have no resident priest.

A churchy megatrend is afoot all right. Whether you like figures or not, all of the above proclaim one message: our numbers are down, lay people and others are filling in. Where it's all going we're not sure, although we'll try to catch a sense of direction in these pages. Meanwhile, we turn to our second megatrend and its tension.

The Second Tension: The decline of the credibility of the need of celibacy as attached to ministry vs. the growth of the charism of marriage. Of late, in both official documents and popular theologizing, much attention has been paid to the dignity and charism of marriage. In fact, the official work is that marriage is now seen as an equal but different path to holiness. This of course is a decided shift from the tradition that celibacy is superior (St. Ambrose), a tradition transmitted to the faithful in its most popular form in the calendar of saints. Even in the revised list, of the 173 saints in the new Roman missal, 145 are men and 28 are women (a statement right there!) but among them 170 are celibates. Contrast this with the survey that indicated that many of the bishops attending Vatican II were open to a married clergy, that lay people, according to a Gallup poll, would welcome a married clergy, that Chicago's Project 1990 survey showed lay leaders very willing to accept married priests, and that a *New York Times*/CBS poll taken in December 1985 showed that almost two-thirds of American Catholics supported the notion of a married clergy. Clearly celibacy as a credible necessity for ordained and nonordained ministry has declined.

Moreover, credible people are saying it now aloud. Cardinal Hume of Westminster, England, has publicly said that married men may have to be ordained priests, as has the current president of the National Conference of Catholic Bishops, Bishop James W. Malone (Youngstown), who said that in extreme situations mandatory celibacy for priests might be abolished. Married Episcopal priests and married Lutheran ministers have been accepted into the Roman communion. All this impacts on the celibate clergy. Not that working side by side with married priestly converts or married deacons, nor the newly appreciated gift of marriage undermines the truly powerful value and witness of celibacy, but these factors do undermine its necessity and the credibility of celibacy for all—a universal necessity which, it is often recalled, did not exist in the first millennium of the church's life.

The Third Tension: The decline of male supremacy and exclusivity vs. the growth of female participation and equality. This particular tension must be seen in the context of the larger feminist movement in society. In the church, women religious are in the forefront demanding equality and full participation they see taking place in other religious traditions. They note, for example, that 50 percent of the students in Protestant seminaries are women (although these candidates find themselves in few full pastorships when they get out). They note too the ending of the dichotomy of men exclusively in the workplace and women exclusively in the home. Women are in fact entering the workplace in large numbers and are bringing family concerns with them. They feel justified in transferring these concerns and experiences to their church.

As a result, women have become more sensitive to discrimination, both in language and policy in the church, and demand that men take note of what they take for granted. For instance, men are asked to put themselves in women's place as they read the taken-for-granted statements in Vatican II documents that all Christians are sons of the one Father, that they have received a spiritual patrimony, that all the members of the church are described only by the masculine pronoun, and that Christians have been called to a universal brotherhood so that fraternal love can shine before all men. Try rereading this aloud to see how you would feel if you were a woman.

How about this woman, an eucharistic minister, who in a letter to a Catholic newspaper, wrote how she felt when she saw people cross over from her line:

> I wonder what you are thinking as you crossed over to Father's line to avoid receiving Communion from me. That I was unworthy to bear the Body of Christ to you? I readily admit that. The priest from whom you receive the eucharist unquestionably is also unworthy. Both of

us have been made acceptable through the saving grace
of him you refuse to accept from my hands...If Christ
was born of a woman, is it not fitting for a woman to
be eucharistic Christ-bearers?...Personally, my hands
feel blessed. They have been trained to nurse the sick.
They have prepared at least 30,000 meals and changed
almost as many diapers. They have spent hours folded
in prayer and in teaching others to pray.

Another woman, a nun, who visits the sick and brings them
communion tells how on one of her visits she prayed with
a very sick man, aware that an old and very sick woman was
in the next bed listening. When she was finished with the
man, Sister went over to say a few words to the woman. The
woman said to her, "Those prayers were beautiful. Tell me,
are you a minister?" Sister was startled for a moment—she
wore a cross, had a badge, seemed "official." It didn't seem
like a time for distinctions so she said, "Yes, I guess I am."
And the old woman smiled, took her arm and said, "I knew
they wouldn't hold our sex against us!" It's the eventual ac-
cumulation of stories like these that keep on challenging the
traditional male supremacy and exclusivity in church matters.

Besides, as Carol Gilligan has shown in her research, men
and women do have different ways of perceiving and speaking about reality, about moral problems, about the way they
describe themselves and their relationships with others. Men
tend to think of themselves in terms of self-identity, to value
freedom, and to judge life by the standards of rights and of
personal achievements. Women tend to think of themselves
in terms of relationships with others or intimacy, to value
equality, and to judge life by the standard of responsibility
and care. Men's center tends to be self and work, and women's
tends to be relationship and people. It would seem, therefore,
that on this pattern alone, women's participation in the church
should be a reality, should be given a rightful platform, if for
no other reason than the balance and the corrective of a *different voice*. In any case, like Paul who co-ministered with
his dear friends Phoebe, Priscilla, and Aquilla we have to re-

spond to (or at least be aware of) the women's challenge to
a church which is, in Elizabeth Schussler-Fiorenza's phrase,
a "discipleship-community of equals."

*The Fourth Tension: The decline of clerical monopoly of power
vs. the growth of shared power with the laity on an equal basis.*
As often noted by sociologists, the trend to centralization and
consolidation of power is a natural impulse of all institutions
both secular and religious. Ultimately there is the need for
institutions to define themselves over and against others and,
along with this, the consequent need to exclude the deviate.
Furthermore, there is a need to have organizational people
keep definitions, teachings, and policies intact and true to their
origins. In the church (all denominations, even if they use
different terminology) we thus see this normal need met in
the tendencies to develop canons, dogmas, rubrics and laws,
and the need to have guardians *(episcopoi)* of the tradition.
But it is also a sociological law that centralizing and exclu-
sion always tend to over-reach ("power corrupts") and go further than they should. The result is that human concerns and
traditions not only start to supersede the gospel and suck in
the legtimate powers and charisms of others but they wind
up skewing the very tradition they are trying to preserve.

For instance, there is in Christian origins an ancient
charismatic strain, the lived belief that the Spirit of God is
radically democratic. This is evidenced on Pentecost Day
when the Spirit was poured out on all indiscriminately. Peter,
in defense of all this does not hesitate to quote the prophet
Joel: "In the last days, God says, I will pour out my Spirit on
all the people" *(Acts 2:17)*. There is, then, a radical equality
of all believers in Christ. In this sense, no one has more power
than another because fundamental empowerment comes from
shared common baptism rather than by singular ordination.
This means that power is a shared reality and that the clergy
have no claim to it exclusively. Where such a claim is made
it will be in contradiction to Vatican II's words: "In Christ and
in the Church there is, then, no inequality arising from race

or nationality or social condition or sex, for there is neither Jew nor Greek; there is neither slave nor freeman; there is neither male nor female, for you are all one in Christ Jesus" *(Gal. 3:28)*.[4]

A newly understood historical consciousness reflected in these words is the reason you get careful statements from leaders like Cardinal Bernardin who says that while "there is an essential difference between ordained and non-ordained ministry, all ministry is rooted in the sacraments of initiation...and there is to be no rivalry, no competition among those with different gifts."[5] So we priests have to come to terms with a more collaborative ministry not because in view of the shortage we have no other choice, but because such collaboration of gifts is rooted in our Sacred Scriptures and tradition.

The Fifth and Final Tension: The decline of the eucharist vs. the growth in the teaching, preaching, and witnessing to the word of God. As the number of priests dwindles, more and more communities are left with other leaders who specialize in the word of God. However, to this extent—already happening in large numbers throughout the world—communities eventually cease to be eucharistic ones. As long as the official line is that the eucharist is confined to ordained male celibates, then the trade-off is basically a substitute form of Protestant word service. This indeed may be effective and gracious but it definitely departs from that ancient Catholic genius summed up in the old rallying slogan of past times, "It's the Mass that matters." Even a word-community fed on previously consecrated communion species led by a deacon or lay minister does not quite capture the tradition. This is a precious heritage to endanger. Unexpected words worth pondering in this regard come from one of Protestantism's most distinguished and influential theologians, Reinhold Niebuhr, long a critic of the Catholic church. He wrote an essay fifteen years after his retirement as professor at Union Theological College in New York and after a stroke had forced him to sit in the pew.

He wrote:

> I had always believed that the vitality of religion after
> the rise of modern science, which tended to discredit
> the legends of religious history, was due to the simple
> fact that faith in an incomprehensible divine source of
> order was an indispensable bearer of the human trust
> in life, despite the evils of nature and the incongruities
> of history. But as I became a pew-worshipper rather than
> a preacher I had some doubts about the ability of us
> preachers to explicate and symbolize this majesty and
> mystery. These pulpit-centered churches of ours, with-
> out a prominent altar, seemed insufficient. Moreover,
> in the nonliturgical churches the 'opening exercises' —
> with a long pastoral prayer which the congregation could
> not anticipate or join in — seemed inadequate. I came to
> view the Catholic Mass, in many religious respects, more
> adequate than our Protestant worship. For the first time
> I ceased to look at Catholicism as a remnant of medieval
> culture. I realized that I envied the popular Catholic
> Mass because that liturgy, for many, expressed the
> mystery which makes sense out of life always threat-
> ened by meaninglessness.[6]

These prophetic words reflect of course our own United States
bishops' words that "the eucharist. . .most fully expresses that
we are called to new relationships with Christ in spite of all
that would separate us. . .In the eucharist the full giving of
all of life in love to God receives its most complete expression." There is truly tension, then, in this last large megatrend
that we are exploring, one that either will trade off a
eucharistic Catholic heritage or find creative ways to ordain
others besides male celibates.

I wonder, too, while we're on this subject, if at the bottom of it all there is not some unconscious fear operating here:
the fear of losing power. You see, the Mass is so central to
Catholic identity that the one presiding at it really is the
ultimate symbol of power. Anything less than presiding at
the eucharist is symbolically unsatisfactory and clearly, in
the Catholic imagination, not full power. True, someone other
than a priest can be a chancellor, judge, pastor, whatever;

but if in the last analysis that person cannot preside at the eucharist—and must call in an outsider to do so—then that person simply is not considered to share in full power no matter how high a position he or she has in the church. On our part, on the hierarchy's part, consciously or unconsciously, we may not want to part with the power we have or even share it at so large a cost. Yet it seems to me that as more and more lay people do move into official ministry, the slow realization will dawn on them that only a few select celibate males do in fact have access both to the real symbolic and actual power in the church at the expense of denied eucharistic celebrations.

At the extraordinary synod in Rome in December 1985, an American woman walked up to an altar in St. Peter's Basilica and simulated saying the Eucharistic Prayer, complete with the consecration, before she was taken away by guards. She was making a statement, as they say, but the statement was not lost on Bishop Malone. As the newspaper account put it, "But Bishop Malone, who supports a larger role for women in the church, acknowledged that by barring women from ordination, Roman Catholicism had excluded them from the traditional sources of church power."[7]

So, there we are: faced with ten megatrends that will affect our lives and the life of the whole church. And here we are, a vanishing species along with the Arctic whale and ibis. And while we are vanishing we have to cope with a professional laity often more educated than ourselves, cope with the loss of status as celibates, as exclusive power brokers, as the one and only source of holiness. This is truly a *kenosis,* an emptying out, but it is precisely here that I detect a compelling gospel echo: Could the anxiety we feel in the face of these megatrends, could our anger and our bewilderment—could all this be the quiet sound and fury that a seed is dying yet yearning to burst forth into something grander? Are we becoming less so that He may become more? Are we, as I am inclined to think we are, in one of those cycles, preparing for an upturn, a new church that really is a people of God

with more resonance to our first century Christian communities than to papal Catholicism? And are we about to rediscover a firmer, more authentic role? I believe we are.

> An elderly woman named Maude had a window seat on the big 747 that has just taken off from New York. She had been scrimping for years to fulfill the dream of a visit to the Eternal City. But it was her first flight ever and she was terrified. Even the presence of four bishops traveling to the Synod did not reassure her. With fear and trembling she finally opened her eyes and peeped out the window just in time to see one of the plane's four engines break loose and disappear into the clouds below. Maude cried out, "We're going to die! We're going to die!" The chief stewardess consulted with the pilot and announced to all the passengers that everything was under control, saying that the captain could fly the plane back to New York on three engines quite safely. But poor, panic stricken Maude continued to cry out, "We're going to die!" The stewardess went to her and said in her best calming voice, "Don't worry, my dear. God is with us. We have only three motors, but look, we have four bishops." "It doesn't matter," cried Maude, "I'd rather have four motors and three bishops!"

*An American priest, dressed in civies, was visiting
Ireland. Suddenly he felt a gun in his back.
"Catholic? Protestant?" demanded the menacing
voice. The priest thought to himself, "If I say
Catholic, he'll surely be Protestant—and vice versa." So he summoned all his shrewdness and
answered, "I'm Jewish." The voice exulted. "I must
be the luckiest Arab in all of Ireland!"*

II

Man in the Middle

IF YOU READ THE LITTLE STORY ABOVE, YOU HAVE SOME IDEA OF THE
theme of this chapter, the priest as Man in the Middle. And
it goes like this: Have I been cursilloed, encountered, renewed, and born again? Am I up on all the latest initials:
RCIA, MACC, CCD, NFF, NCCB, NALR, NFPC? The Natural
Family Planning Course, the Knights of Columbus, the Holy
Name, Rosary Altar, the school, the Boy Scouts, the Liturgy
Committee, and the Girl Scouts all want me to be present
on the same day and at the same time. It's the month of Right
to Life, the Rosary, vocations, the family, as well as first communion and confirmation. The mail on my desk wants my
time and my money to save orphans, feed the hungry, ran-
som babies, run a university, and heal lepers. Next to the
mountainous mail are notes from those who want to see me,
both parishioners and the great anonymous unwashed who

21

were given my name. Alongside the notes are notices from
the pope, the bishop, the chancellor, and the personnel director. Beside the notices are announcements of seminars,
workshops, conventions, and conferences. In front of them
all is the parish book with its summons to funerals, weddings,
baptisms, and sick calls and meetings—endless, ongoing
meetings at which there is almost sheer mathematical cer-
tainty we shall die. Or, as Father John Heagle says, when the
Parousia arrives, we'll be at a meeting.

And the questions: Father, why aren't more people march-
ing in the streets, sending aid to Ethiopia, protesting abor-
tions? Why is our parish mission so poorly attended? Why
don't you have a Catholic school? Why haven't we any vocations in this parish (heavy implications of personal failure
here)? Why don't you promote the rosary, Blue Army,
scapular, etc.? Going away *again*, Father? And, why don't you
relax and take some time off? You look tired.

There is no doubt about it, the average Catholic pastor
is the last of the GPs. In the course of a week he will, without
skipping a beat, talk to the second grade, counsel someone
considering an abortion, drop in on the senior citizens, speak
at all the Masses, give a talk to the local Lion's Club, sign
checks, look at the toilet which is backed up again, replace
light bulbs, and be asked his considered opinion about solv-
ing the problem of the homeless in the nuclear age. No
wonder one priest described the pastor's job as doing
everything no one else wants to do and yet must be done.
"When the diocese raises taxes or fees, when the utility companies raise their rates, when the parish committees raise their
budgets, when the government increases Social Security rates
or cuts poverty programs, where does it all end up? On the
pastor's desk, in the pastor's worries. . . .[1] As Joe Gallagher
wrote in his book, *The Pain and the Promise: The Diary of a
City Priest*, "I can recall one afternoon in my life when I ab-
solved penitents in the confessional, baptised a premature
baby at Maryland General, anointed a ninety-year old woman

dying in her dingy room, celebrated the Eucharist, and joined in holy wedlock two starry-eyed lovers."[2]

Such general practioner stuff, over the years, is bound to bring about burnout and stress. No one, in spite of St. Paul, can be all things to all men – much less women – all the time. That we are not succeeding is verified by a recent study by a committee of U.S. bishops which shows that while 83.6 percent of U.S. priests describe their health as excellent, 39.5 percent reported "severe personal or mental problems" in the previous twelve months. Should we mention here also that the number of clergy who die before retirement has doubled in recent years? Stress is obviously catching up with us. Still, we could possibly manage or get back on a better track if it weren't for the fact that they suddenly changed the rules on us. "They," of course, means society in general and Vatican II in particular. It's one thing to struggle when you know the game plan and it's quite another when you don't even know what the game itself is anymore.

For one thing, there are entirely new needs to be taken care of that were not a part (very much anyway) of the old clerical scene: ministry to the divorced, the singles, aged, Hispanics, the homeless, and gays. There are entirely new issues to be mastered: civil disobedience, nuclear disarmament, apartheid, and the economy. As Archbishop Roger Mahony of Los Angeles said to his priests:

> What is expected from a priest has mounted to unmanageable proportions: new forms of liturgical celebrations, the latest skills in working with many new consultative groups, a honed knowledge of American nuclear weaponry, an economic sophistication sufficient enough to understand the U.S. Catholic bishops' new pastoral letter on the economy, the demand for updating in theology and scripture, many new linguistic skills being required, and the problems of increasingly large parish communities. . . . And add to this the experience that almost everything within our life lies open to question. [3]

The real panic sets in when we realize that all these new expectations have not replaced the old ones but have simply been added to them. It's not hard to figure the equation: more and different expectations plus fewer priests equals burnout. Father Tom Ventura's 1990 Chicago project surveyed twenty-three representative parishes and found that pastors do experience a "growing tension from being the man in the middle between the church above and the church below; between old and new expectations, between conservatives and liberals, between staff members and/or lay volunteers who get involved in 'turf' fights." In the past the pastor had high moral authority to deal with all this, but this too has eroded. He now has to earn respect and obedience. Among 157 pastors in Chicago Tom Ventura found a sense of being underdogs with no real power or financial rewards. When they were associates such pastors could at least look forward to both. Now ironically that they have arrived at this stage of ecclesiastical history they suddenly find that they must share them.

Moreover, the egalitarian approach of the priesthood of all the faithful (the people of God) makes the pastor feel more than ever that he has a lot of responsibility but no real power, no real structure to accomplish what has to be done. For years he was *the* community minister. Now he is apt to ask himself, "If people who aren't ordained can do many of the things I do, what is the meaning of my priesthood? How am I different? What difference does ordination make?" Then, too, in the past, the priest knew he could hold his own in the community. He worked long and hard to get through the seminary and get his degree. He was right up there with the doctors and the lawyers. Now he finds himself working with people who are far more updated, educated, and degreed than himself. Professional envy, status, power, identity—all are assaulted to some degree or other for the man in the middle.

A recent Public Television documentary followed a priest from the last months of the seminary to the first months of parish life. The program showed quite clearly that the priest is a man who is expected to deal competently with every conceivable situation – and cheerfully at that, any time of the day or night. The young priest expressed the frustration of all when, in the light of his short hectic experience, he exclaimed that people still were of the opinion that he didn't do much after he said Mass. It's the old dig, said smilingly, "All through, Father, till next weekend?" The proper response, after supressing the impulse to kick the questioner in the groin, is, "Yes. It's an easy life. That's why the seminaries are empty. No one wants an easy life anymore." This ranks in the same league with the cartoon I saw showing the priest on his knees in his office saying his prayers, and the cleaning lady barges in and says. "Oh, good. I thought you might have been doing something." This is only one notch above the parishioner who phones and hears your answer that you're working on your homily and says with relief, "Oh, good, since you're not busy I'll come right over." Shades of dialogue, discernment and interface!

As you suspect, we're not through yet. All of this might be tolerable (just might be) to some degree except for the singular lack of affirmation from our "father figures," the Big Three Cs: Council, Code, and Chancery. While the Vatican council did marvelous work in honing and increasing the identity and power of the bishops, and while it gave over a whole section of its interest to the laity, nothing significant was said about the position of the pastor beyond the usual exhortations. He, the pastor, is an extension of the bishop (something like being perennial vice-president); he has no union, no lobby to speak for him. As far as his role in the new church goes, the council was silent and left him with bold new terrain, but no map. The hierarchy, when it got back home from the council, gave him no concerted or in-depth preparation for post-Vatican implementation. The pastor had to bear the brunt of explaining, on the street level, changes that were often handed or mailed to him without the slightest hint of what it was all about or how to handle it pastorally. He was once more the Man in the Middle, ill prepared to understand the official church and teach the people in the pews and where, in all of this, he stood himself. He could readily identify with Jesus: And Jesus saith unto them, "And who do you say that I am?" And they replied, "You are the escatological manifestation of the ground of being, the kerygma of our interpersonal relationship, the existential metaphor in which we subsist." And Jesus saith unto them, *"What?"*

Father Rawley Myers in a letter to *America* wrote:

> Thanks to the brilliant Monica Hellwig for stating in her essay on the extraordinary synod (9/28) that "a discussion by select bishops is not an adequate instrument for the evaluation of Vatican II."

> When will we learn that the Catholic church is the parish? All kinds of meetings can be created on high, but if they are not implemented on the parish level (the heart of the church) nothing happens. The parish priest is the key to this and both Vatican Council II and the postconciliar church largely ignored him. Until he is seriously consulted, the church will continue to spin its wheels.

The Revised Code of Canon Law did the same thing as the council: it made provisions for bishops and gave the laity a whole section of rights and power but remained silent on any new role for pastors, any strong guidelines on how to pastor in a new age with a new agenda.

As far as the average chancery goes, that code word for the bishop and his attendees, stories of indifference and taken-for-grantedness are legendary, as every priest knows—although the following commentary must be softened with many instances of sensitive chanceries and personnel, especially in these days of current crisis. But for some the old assumed principal was that pastors existed for the chancery and all of its multiplying departments, not the other way around. Sink or swim was the unspoken motto, and you were for the most part left alone barring any scandalous (usually concerning doctrine, not conduct) affair. We were expected to live over the store, see to it that services were

provided, and be financiers, administrators, and school super-
visors whether or not we had natural talent, for there was
no training whatsoever in these areas. There was no
camaraderie, no personal visit from the bishop (confirmation
time didn't count, it was official) on a man to man, priest to
priest basis. There was never any sense of belonging to a
presbyterate since, as American men, we were left with the
Marlboro solitary man ideal. Rivalries, yes; cooperation, no.
Problems with alcohol, sex, and overwork were left to take
care of themselves.

In the summer of 1985 the *National Catholic Reporter* ran
an article exposing priest pedophiles. The unsavory article
outraged many, as well it might. Such items are best left to
be worked out in the private domain rather than aired as dirty
clerical laundry for all the world to see—especially when
clergy morale and image are at an all time low. Still, as anx
ious and ambivalent as I was over that public exposure, I
could see why it surfaced. I knew of several cases where the
bishop did know of such happenings but simply moved a
clerical pedophile from one assignment to another, usually
to wind up in charge of altar boys or the Boy Scouts. Such
gross neglect and indifference usually spawns more dramatic
responses such as the *Reporter* article in the interest of justice,
for there was no doubt that basically injustice was being
condoned.

The problem has in fact become so sensitive—with more
than 40 cases in the last two years against priests—that in the
spring of 1986 more than 100 church officials from the East
Coast met in New Jersey to discuss the problem both from
the legal point of view (one case in Louisiana may cost the
insurance company and diocese ten million dollars, with insurance companies in many other places cancelling in cases
of sexual abuse by priests) and an ethical point of view. Said
one lawyer, "The Roman Catholic Church cannot credibly ex-
ert moral authority externally in any area where the public
perceives it as incapable of maintaining moral authority internally."

More to the issue, it points up that at times some chanceries can be ignorant of their men's needs and so fail to reach out with genuine help and healing. Frequently too, chanceries fail to reward or to recognize their clerical prophets—those who often work in the trenches and who could use a little encouragement, affirmation, and public approval.

We are now, of course, in what could be called a sellers market. Bishops are beginning to realize the value of this graying, vanishing species and so there have been all kinds of programs designed for the care and feeding of the clergy:

> While war and peace and justice and the U.S. economy were the prime issues at the meeting of the Catholic bishops in Washington, D.C. last week, the status and well-being of the nation's Catholic priests were never far from the minds of prelates and their advisors. Although the exodus of priests from the active ministry has dropped to a trickle, vocations are not sufficient to replace the ravages of death and retirement. Thus a sensation of strain and frustration seems endemic among many of the younger clerics. It is causing concern among the prelates. . . . A drive is on to reinvest the priesthood with the aura of adventure, commitment to solving people's personal problems, while ministering the word of God with competence and wit.[4]

Much remains to be done certainly and, in the context of our discussion, probably the best boon to a renewed and recovered priesthood is the election of pastoral bishops who should be required by law to have the skills of leadership and inspiration. Ah, well, it's an old problem. Reaching back in our ecclesiastical history we pluck out this item. In February 1878, the Irish bishop George Conroy, who was the apostolic delegate to Canada, arrived in the United States on an official visit. After extensive travel around the country, he submitted his report to Rome taking the pains to mention that bishops were too frequently chosen because of qualities, in his words, more proper "to a banker and not the Pastor of souls," and in turn the bishops seem to use the same criteria in appointing priests to the missions. The more things change. . . .

Now hear this: the dutiful pastor began doing volunteer work rehabilitating former mental patients. He often visited a large mental institution where he interviewed patients who were about to be discharged, helping them to explore job opportunities. On one such visit, the pastor encountered a man who was going to be discharged in two weeks. The patient was busy building a brick wall in front of one of the buildings. After a long conversation the pastor asked, "Would you like to come to do some work for me at the parish?" The patient enthusiastically replied that he would like that very much. "Fine," said Father, "I must go now but I'll return Monday and speak to the superintendent about it." Then as he turned and began to walk around toward the gate, the priest was struck by a brick thrown at his head. Stunned, he fell to the ground. When he looked up he saw the patient happily waving to him as he shouted, "You won't forget Monday, will you?"

The story is my way of saying we have one or two more bricks to take on the head before we take a look at some really good news. One brick says that nowadays, besides having more expectations and fewer priests, being caught in the middle and being somewhat (at least in the past) taken for granted or unappreciated by our father figures, we can now also be sued for false advice and may be pressured into breaking the confessional seal if we are privy to a case of child abuse in California, Texas, or Florida. How's that to make us feel further appreciated?

It's that last word, appreciated, that leads us to our final brick. There is some interesting data on priests' psychological adjustment that has been collected in the past twenty years in relation to what is called the 16PF, a sixteen point comparison of personality traits devised about thirty years ago by a Dr. Raymond Cattell and his associates. It just so happened that some 1,707 Catholic priests were included in the overall sampling of American men and most of them showed

great similarity with the general run of the American male—
except in one significant category in which they were
dramatically different. The Catholic priest was extremely
"tender-minded," that is, he was unusually kind and gentle,
had a real need to be needed, and wanted and expected very
much attention and gratitude for his efforts.

In short, the tests showed that priests were really very
compassionate people (which led them to the ministry to begin
with) but ones who also had a strong need to be appreciated
for their efforts. Typically the priest is one who has a strong
desire to help others but who expects to get an affectionate
response from those so helped. He needs recognition and
thanks for reaching out. Similar data from the Myers- Briggs
Type Indicator show that clergy tend by far to make choices
based on feeling rather than thinking and that pastors who
want to please do expect a reward for their efforts and get
outraged when it's not forthcoming.

In times past, this need was amply fulfilled. The im-
migrant church of the last century clearly needed the priest
who represented the old country's religion, customs, and
rituals. Priests were needed for all of the sacraments and were
close to the people, who responded to them for the most part
with genuine affection and respect. Families considered it an
honor to be visited by the priest or to have a relative or son
who was all one. All that has changed, of course. American
Catholics are no longer immigrants: they are now in the
mainstream, well off, well educated, independent, and pretty
much indistinguishable from their non-Catholic counterparts
in values, attitudes, and lifestyles. They no longer need a
priest and his schools and ethnic parishes to get them accepted
into society. They no longer see the priesthood, as we have
noted, as a viable or desirable career. So, not needed as of
old, "undermined" by an active laity (the movement, as we
shall see, from a "Father" church to a "Spirit" community),their
celibate lives publicly questioned, their confreres resigning,
Mass attendance down, vocations dried up, feeling what they

call a "lack of personal fulfillment," no wonder a pervasive sense of being unappreciated and unneeded – the heart of their emotional well being – overcomes them and undermines their morale.

Priests react. Father Joseph Krastel, who has noted these conditions says that they simply find other ways to be needed.[5] They take courses all over the place, especially in counseling, figuring that since people no longer go to them for confession, they might come in for counseling. Or they move into social action and social work or teaching, anywhere where the people are. Another phenomenon is noted by Father Krastel, priests' preaching has changed. Very few sermons are heard in the land about the hard aspects of the Christian life and morality. No more thundering sermons about indecent dress or X-rated movies or birth control or the pains of hell. No strong sermons on social justice. Why? Because the priest, sensing his devaluation, doesn't want to alienate, to create any more distance from himself. After all, he needs to be needed and appreciated.

There is an ironic bottom line to this whole chapter. It is within the megatrend context of declining numbers, overwork, eroding identity, devalued lifestyle, yet needing to be needed that the priest of today is asked to be a collaborator in ministry – which is something like asking the lead player with an ailing throat to pray fervently for the success of his understudy! The poor priest, the man in the middle.

Many a priest was afraid of the former and formidable Archbishop Curley of Baltimore. "Once a nervous master of ceremonies put the mitre backward on Curley's head, so that the wide, long flaps fell down over the prelate's face. "Stand back," Curley is said to have commanded, "and let everyone see what a nincompoop you are!"
Perhaps it was this same ill-fated cleric who on

another occasion forgot to put the mitre on
Curley. "Put the mitre on! Put the mitre on!"
barked the archbishop. The priest was so rattled
that he obeyed by putting the mitre on his own
head. [Joe Gallagher, in The Pain and the
Promise]

I am plagued by doubts. What if everything is an illusion and nothing exists? In that case, I definitely overpaid for the carpet. If only God would give me some clear sign: like making a large deposit in my name at a Swiss bank.
(Woody Allen)

III

Good News

"OKAY," SAID THE TEACHER, "WE'VE GONE OVER THE MATERIAL IN THE past weeks, so now, a little review." Then she paused, looked at the class, and spat out, " 'Give me liberty or give me death.' Who said that?" Funereal silence until a little Japanese boy, Fugimoto, raised his hand and said, "Patrick Henry, March 23, 1775." "Correct," said the teacher, "very good, very good indeed," as she surveyed the rest of the class with contempt. "All right," she continued. "'Four score and seven years ago.' Who said that?" Again total silence, and again Fugimoto raised his hand and said, "Abraham Lincoln, November 19, 1863." The teacher acknowledged the correct answer with a nod as she looked on the others with even more scorn. "Well," she exclaimed, "all of you were born here. Your parents were born here and nobody seems to know anything about his own native land except Fugimoto. Very well, then. Since you know so little about your own country, we're going to have a test. Take out a sheet of paper and answer these questions." Amid

33

the groans, the teacher turned to write the test questions on
the blackboard. And, while her back was turned, there was
one of those loud stage whispers as someone exclaimed,
"Those g.d. Japanese!" The teacher spun around. "All right.
I heard that remark. Who said that?" Silence. Once again
Fugimoto raised his hand, "Harry Truman, August 3, *1947!*"

So, we're bad off. Our numbers are down, seminarians
are practically on the endangered list, everything's going
downhill. Who said that? Most everyone. But are things really
that bad? Is there no good news to cheer our clerical hearts?
True, the statistics of the first chapter are foreboding, but,
put in a different context, do they necessarily spell doom?
Is there a way of putting things in a different perspective
without going pollyanna or denying the present crisis or the
future challenge? Is there room for hope. The answer is yes
and that's the burden of this chapter: to explore some credible signs of the clerical times that bespeak opportunity,
challenge, and cause for joy.

Let's start with those statistics. They do indeed indicate
a shortage of priests, both now and in the future, as many
dioceses know from current anxious experience. There *are*
fewer seminarians in our country. We will have many fewer
replacements for ourselves. Nevertheless, any statement
about a priest or seminarian shortage must be expressed this
way: there is a shortage, true, but a shortage relative to what?
The only sensible answer is, relative to the needs of the people, which is the only real, practical criterion to go by.[1]
Nobody seems to look at the angle, just as nobody has ever
really established, for each country's temperament and needs,
just how many priests per population are needed to provide
effective leadership and community. The answers will
obviously vary. For instance, consider this case: there is now
one priest for every 4000 people, where there used to be, let's
say, one priest for every 2000 people. This sudden doubling
is indeed a challenge. But take the same case and add some
details. There is that one priest plus two deacons, eight professional ministers, and lots of involved lay ministry. Now,

what does the word "shortage" tell us? Obviously it's going to take on a different coloring, a relative meaning. There certainly is a shortage in the first version, but in the second, in relation to the needs of the people, that's debatable.

Or you may want to consider one indifferent and ineffective priest per 1000 people versus one involved and effective priest per same 1000 people. Where does "shortage" occur? You see, if you position the priest/seminarian shortage in the context of fulfilling the needs of people, in terms of quality over quantity, in terms of possible shared and collaborative ministry, then it's not as bad as it first seems. Or, let me express it another way. We said in Chapter One that by the year 2000, according to all projections, there will likely be a ratio of one priest for every 4000 people in the United States. Right now that ratio runs about one priest for every 1000 people. The addition of 3000 more to the ratio is not totally disasterous if you project the strong likelihood of increased shared ministry.

What could also be operating here is our own cultural, consumer biases. Look at the other continents. In 1982, according to the *Statistical Yearbook of the Church* (Rome, December 1982), there was one priest for every 27,731 Catholics in Asia and for every 239,137 Catholics in Europe. As for seminarians, it is true that we in this country have far less of them to replace the current crop of priests and we in the United States have experienced the largest decrease in their numbers, more than anywhere else on the planet. On the other hand, it is sobering to note that other continents have witnessed *significant increases* in seminarians, especially in Asia, Africa, and Latin America. The point is that when we consider the needs of the people and when we add in the consideration of quality, when we (rightly) anticipate much fuller shared and collaborative lay ministry and can anticipate missionaries from other countries (in a neat historical reversal), then the picture does not seem so bleak. It's not bright, but this is another perspective to the priest shortage and a more hopeful one at that. And that's good news.

Second, in relationship to the priest shortage, there are some possible solutions which I would share here just to point up that it's not the unbearable weight we think it is. Now honesty demands that you and I admit that not all these solutions are currently acceptable—though most are. Still, every one of them is theoretically, theologically, and historically possible. If our crises continue, I suspect we will see some of them as realities sooner than we think. Anyway, I'll list ten such possibilities.

1. *Ordain married men.* Recall Bishop Malone's view that in "extreme situations mandatory celibacy for priests might be abolished." We are all aware that the official and final ban on married priests is traceable to the Lateran Council of 1139 in the West and that the East has always permitted a married clergy. We saw in previous chapters that the Catholic church has welcomed married clerical converts and has ordained married deacons. This first possibility is therefore no stranger to most people. In fact, it's an acceptable, comfortable, and *preferred* thought. Dean Hoge from Catholic University has researched this question and found that among both conservative and liberal Catholics the desire for their priests was so strong that it overrode current rules about married men being ineligible.

Again, we might ponder the specter of losing our identity as a eucharistic church if there are not enough celibate priests to go around. I'm thinking, for example, of a veteran African missionary writing in Britain's *Clergy Review*, citing that the Africa's church membership over the past twenty-five years has grown 300 percent and, despite a high vocation and ordination rate, the numbers of priests are not able to keep pace. The results, he points out, are that many Catholic communities, dependent as they are on lay catechists, are becoming little different from those of their Protestant neighbors. He sees ordaining married men as the only way to keep the church eucharistic in Africa.

2. *Reinstate the priests already married.* It is estimated that anywhere from 70,000 to 100,000 priests have gotten married since Vatican II and many of them had no desire to part with the church. Others, of course, have no desire to return since they left, not over celibacy, but over other institutional difficulties. Still, when former priests met in Rome in the summer of '85, the group, calling themselves The Universal Synod of Married Catholic Priests and Their Wives, declared their desire to return to an active ministry. As one of their organizers reminded the group (and the Vatican), "The priesthood and matrimony are not in *opposition,* and in the history of the church they were united for centuries." He also took pains to point out that the group recognized the great value of celibacy—they had no wish to denegrate that—as well as that of marriage, but they were simply seeking an optional celibacy for the Western priests that the Eastern ones have enjoyed. Recall once more, too, that the polls show the laity in general, many of the bishops, and four-fifths of the priests themselves open to a married clergy. In fact, the United States bishops in their September 1985 Report on Roman Catholicism in the post-Vatican II era, written in preparation for the synod of that year, wrote, "The shortage of new priestly vocations requires specifically addressing such issues as celibacy and the general weakening of the sense of commitment apparent in our culture today."

3. *Free up clerical officials.* We noted how the cardinal of New York moved his priests out of chancery work into the parishes. There are many administrative jobs that do not require an ordained cleric who should be freed up for parish work.

4. *Redistribute the manpower.* This is an ally of the above. Some parishes and dioceses have more than they need while others languish. There may have to be serious local and regional redistribution of priests.

5. *Extend the service of the retired.* One bishop, Bishop Higi of Lafayette, Indiana, has a program of keeping senior clergy in service with full status (and salaries) as pastors but without administrative duties. Many senior priests still want to keep their hand in things but without the burden of management.

6. *Prepare foreign imports now.* Just importing priests from other countries with good will is not enough, if they cannot relate to the American cultural scene, celebrate, or most of all, preach well in our idiom. Since the clerical mathematics are clearly with the other countries, then surely the preparation for some long-range exchange program on a large scale could be put into effect now. It seems to me that some serious indoctrination should be going on now to prepare for the importation of ready and culturally honed community builders here in this country.

7. *Institute limited service.* Ordination to the priesthood need not imply that one can *never* change careers later on. This can be done in spite of the popular misconception that if the priest can leave the priesthood, I can leave my marriage. (Marriage permanancy comes from God. Career priesthood permanancy comes from the church.) No divine law covers the permanent priestly career. Being a priest "forever" according to the order of Melchisedech is as tenuous as that mysterious gentleman himself. Ordination is a call from the church and need not be forever – or at least in its public practice. Or, perhaps to put it more softly and precisely, one can be a priest forever, but one need not practice that ministry all his life but may, at a certain point in his life, honorably take on another. A general may retire with honor from the military and take up other work. Even a president and a pope may resign and take up other work – and have. Peace Corps volunteers or mission volunteers may serve with heroism and dignity for years and then leave for other occupations without shame. Why should it be different for the priesthood? What is to prevent a young man, yes, even a celibate young man, from promising ten or twenty years to church service with

the option of either renewing his vows or opting honorably for another occupation (and marriage) later on? As Father Richard McBrien points out:

> Ecclesiology does not support the notion that the priest is a kind of other worldly, almost mystical figure, superior to all non-ordained Christians, with a relationship to God that would be sullied by human love and sexual intimacy . . . The priesthood is, first and foremost, a ministry – a way of assisting the Church to fulfill its missionary mandate to preach, to worship, to witness and to serve – in the name of Jesus Christ, through the power of the Holy Spirit, for the sake of the Kingdom of God. And this ministry need not be for life.[2]

8. *Widen the powers of the ordained permanent deacons.* There is no historical reason why, for example, a deacon could not anoint the sick or even hear confessions under certain circumstances. Both of these would take a great burden off the parish priests and chaplains and incidentally provide for a much more consistent and powerful presence in our hospitals, nursing homes and senior citizen villages, a witness in which we are far behind our Protestant confreres.

9. *Recruit older men to become priests.* This recommendation came from the extensive 1985 survey of Catholic college students, adults and priests sponsored by the Lilly Endowment. In a few dioceses this is already taking place. Second careers for longer living men who might be retired or widowed are becoming commonplace and so this is an area to explore. Also, young adults in their 30s and 40s are turning more and more to second careers and a reach out to them would be profitable.

10. *Ordain (celibate) women.* (The celibacy is a concession to easement.) Of all the suggestions this is currently a closed issue as we all know and likely will be for some time to come. Nevertheless, there is no harm in making some quick reflections here. One reflection is that the question is not as modern as we like to think. "At the same time I want to be a priest." Who said that? This is sure to trip up anyone playing Catholic

Trivia. The author of that saying is St. Theresa, the Little Flower, and she wrote that in her autobiography. Moreover, in June 1897, just three months before her death, she said to her sister Celine:

> Don't you see that God is going to take me at an age when I would not have had time to become a priest. If I had been able to become a priest, it would have been in this month of June, at this ordination, that I would have received holy orders. So in order that I may regret nothing, God is allowing me to be sick. I wouldn't have been able to present myself for ordination, and would have died before exercising my ministry.[3]

To the Catholic St. Theresa of the last century, let's add the thoughts of a Baptist seminary professor of this century who remarks on his experience in teaching women:

> The best students I have in Southern Seminary are women. They've got better minds and better backgrounds. They are better at preparing sermons than anyone else I have in class. And yet the most ill-prepared, uncommitted, limited man has a better chance for ministry in our denomination than some of the most brilliant people I teach. Until the pulpits of this land begin to deal with that, we are wasting not just half our gifts, we are wasting probably 60 percent of our gifts.[4]

Of course, as everyone knows, our Catholic tradition on the matter is summed up in the 1976 declaration of the Congregation for the Doctrine of the Faith called *Inter Insignores* which said, "The church, in fidelity to the example of the Lord, does not consider herself authorized to admit women to priestly ordination." This is indeed an authorative statement, but it is not infallible. To that extent it leaves the question open. To the extent that it is open these words written in 1971 can still be valid: "It is historically more accurate to speak of a nontradition concerning the ordination of women rather than a tradition against it." [5]

Any of these suggestions, even the mildest ones, will require some adaptations, but in fact we have always really adapted to them anyway. We have had priests with full-time secular occupations (the tentmaker from Tarsus) and married priests (the fisherman from Galilee), and nonfunctioning ones (Richelieu, Tallyrand). Even now we are comfortable with the so called hyphenated priests: the priest-scientist, the priest-principal, the priest-teacher, etc., who in effect have no parish community and give little time to it beyond weekend help. They are in reality part-time priests with most of their energy devoted, not to preaching or worshiping, but to the full careers of caretaking, continuing education, conferences, and so on. In any case, the whole point of this section is to emphasize the good news that there are some creative solutions to the priest shortage that only want vision and imagination to come into existence and make our day. We are not doomed to permanent paralysis. There are responses and possibilities which are acceptable to more of the faithful than we probably think.

This, in fact, was an important finding in the Project 1990 of the Archdiocese of Chicago. When people were asked about their views of the future in regard to priests, these results were quoted in *The Chicago Catholic* (April 12, 1985, p. 15): The message was clear. The leaders were saying, "We need and want full time priests to serve us, whether they are celibate, male, or not. In short: there is not shortage of vocations to the priesthood, but only to the qualifications. . . which have been set." The report states that the desire to ordain married men and women to the priesthood was found in both the liberal-minded and conservative-minded parishes.

The third piece of good news is that in spite of change and considerable postcouncil chaos, the fact is that we belong to an institution that in general enjoys much public esteem and confidence. Did you know that a September 1985 Gallup poll noted that, as in all the years since 1973, public confidence in church or organized religion is higher than any other key institutions of our society: more than television, big business, or the public school? The Notre Dame Study on parish life reports that more than half the people spoke favorably of our homilies and 85 percent say that the parish

serves their spiritual needs in some way beyond the Sunday
Mass. The Princeton Religion Research Center in October
1985 proclaimed a headline which read, "Doctors, clergy have
most 'prestigious' jobs." Alvin Illig's Evangelization Center's
survey in late 1985 reports that 85 percent of unchurched
Catholics say they find other teachings of the church attractive (birth control, abortion, use of money are "unattractive"
teachings) as well as the church's sense of family that provides emotional and moral support. "This is one of the most
significant findings of the survey," said George Gallup, who
conducted the survey for Illig's center. "The Roman Catholic
church is clearly offering something Americans today earnest-
ly seek—supportive and dependable fellowship. Americans
are among the loneliest people in the world and seek community." Four in ten of the unchurched say they have thought of
rejoining the church."

Finally, we should note William McCready's words (director of the cultural pluralism program of the National Opinion
Research Center at the University of Chicago): "The American
Catholic laity are among the 'most Catholic' in the world. Their
rates of attendance at Mass are still among the highest in the
world. They remain loyal to their religious heritage. And yet
they feel they can criticize official church positions without
sacrificing that loyalty."

Let's include Andrew Greeley's observation from
American Catholics Since the Council: An Unauthorized Report
which affirms that, again in spite of much upheaval in the
church, studies and surveys *consistently* show among all
segments of the Catholic populace that priests are still of enormous importance to Catholics. He adds:

> Though American Catholics may complain about seling
> the quality of preaching and the quality of counselling
> and sensitivity they encounter in the rectory, they still
> have considerable respect for the sincerity and the
> diligence, if not the professional competence, of their
> priests. . . . Admiration and respect for parish priests was
> still high. Moreover, the most powerful single influence
> in facilitating the return of someone to the church who

had drifted away – particularly a young Catholic in early and middle twenties – was a relationship with a priest.[6]

That says a lot about us, and we should savor it.

Allied to the general good esteem in which we are held is an increasing regard for our "product." The newspapers lately have been proclaiming headlines like these from *The New York Times:* "Students Turning to Spiritual Life at Campuses in New York Area" (December 25, 1985), and "Religion Plays Growing Role on Campuses" (January 5, 1986). The articles note that college students are turning to organized religion in large numbers, enrolling in religion courses, attending services in significantly increasing numbers, volunteering for charity work, and shucking the "me" generation image – and all this in those Northeast colleges and universities long noted for their secularism and agnosticism.

Then there are unexpected statements like the following:

> I've always believed in God, though I have no formal religion. That is another of my regrets. I have always loved the sense of peace I felt when I went into church. . . . I wish I had given my children what I didn't have, because I think being brought up with a formal religion gives a structure and ritual to our beliefs – a way to think about the great issues of life, such as what is life's purpose and what are our responsibilities as human beings.

That's from someone you associate with exercise, acting, and social activism: Jane Fonda being interviewed in the October 1985 issue of *Ladies Home Journal.* Then there's playwright and author, Dan Wakefield, who after many years as an atheist, decided to go back to church. He writes:

> To my surprise, I recognized neighbors and even some people I considered friends at church . . . yet there they were, with intellects intact, worshipping God. . . .
>
> Going to church, even belonging to it, did not solve life's problems – if anything they seemed to intensify around this time – but it gave me a sense of living in a larger context, of being part of something greater than what I could

see through the tunnel vision of my personal concerns. . . . I experienced what is a common phenomenon
for people who in some way or other began a journey
of the kind I so unexpectedly found myself on—a feeling simply and best described as a "thirst" for spiritual
understanding and contact; to put it bluntly, I guess, for
God.[7]

Andrew Greeley's sociological studies have shown that
especially among the young when they get married or start
a family there is a measurable return to the faith. So we have
something to offer. We *are* a living sign of invitation and
meaning and, yes, sought-after counterculture.

Fourth, the good news says that history has a leveling
message for those of us who are crying woe is me, things have
never been so bad. The perverse good news is that things *have*
been worse, and we have not only survived but prospered.
The priesthood has seen some deplorable situations from
which it has sprung back gloriously. It is our own confrere
and gracious historian John Tracy Ellis who with authority
reminds us:

> The Catholic Church has been no stranger to departures
> from the priesthood, beginning with the son of God's loss
> of one of the original 12 he himself chose as priests. Nor
> has any period in the church's nearly 2000 years of life
> been spared that sad happening. For example, once
> Luther had made his break others followed and by
> November, 1521, of the 40 members of his own Witten-
> burg friary, 15 had left.

Again, Ellis shares with us a letter from Peter Canisius
in that same century who complains, "Young men no longer
care for the priesthood. From what I hear on every hand, in
the space of 20 years scarcely have two students of the university been ordained." Does that four-hundred-year-old observation sound familiar? Ellis further quotes an English historian
of that same era who noted that "many monks and nuns and
friars walked out of their houses apparently without batting
an eye." And then there is the apostolic nuncio writing to Cardinal Consolve, Pius VII's Secretary of State, in 1817: "The

fact is that the clergy in the vast domains of His Imperial Majesty present a truly horrible aspect. They are extremely scarce and insufficient to provide for the needs of the people. "Again, doesn't all this sound familiar, like something from the 1980s? Let's listen to Ellis one more time:

> When you and I are tempted to grow discouraged by such all too real phenomena as the continuing departures from the priesthood, the stark decline in priestly vocations. . . our spirits can be lifted by the remembrance of far greater storms that the church has ridden out in its nearly 2000 years in this world. Moreover, we can be heartened by the words of our co-religionists in other lands spoken amid the encircling darkness of the Catholic community. When, for example, the French church was caught in the grip of a stridently anti-clerical government in the opening years of this century, Father Charles deFoucauld wrote to his friend, Msgr. Maxime Caron, rector of the minor seminary of Versailles, in June 1909, and said: "Don't be troubled by the present storms; the barque of Peter has weathered many another. Think of the evening of the day when St. Peter and St. Paul were martyred; how dark everything must have seemed to the little Christian community of Rome. The first Christians were not discouraged. But we can strengthen our faith with the memory of 18 centuries of the life of the church; how vain and empty then seem the present attempts of the powers of hell, of whom Jesus said, "They will not prevail."[8]

Our fifth bit of good news may appear to slip into some unseemly, unecumenical attitudes, but it is not meant that way. It's just that we contemplate our own bad news so often and so long that we are sure that by comparison the friendly Protestant competition is doing so much better. After all, they have all those vocations and all those married clergy and that fantastic priesthood of all the faithful. Well, I think we ought to look more carefully at the comparison and that oversupply of Protestant clergy and priesthood of all the people to realize that we're not that bad off, that both camps have more problems in common than we think.

There are indeed many Protestant clergypeople, more than enough of them, in fact. On the other hand, this over-supply poses its particular problem, because the mainline churches are in a severe decline. Take, for example, the Episcopal church. Their numbers have dropped 25 percent since 1966, while during the same period their seminarians and clergy are numerous and holding. So much so that one of their wags has predicted if people keep on entering the seminary and others drop out of church, by the year 2000 there should be one clergy for every lay person! The Lutherans also have current oversupply of clergy, but some worry that by the year 1990 declining enrollment in their seminaries plus expected retirements will produce a shortage. Oversupply also produces its own problems, namely lack of jobs. Right now 371 Lutheran candidates for the ministry are still awaiting a call. And even though some Protestant denominations ordain women, many of the women (most?) do not receive major pastorships.

And what about their vaunted reliance on "Scripture alone" which neatly resolves all of the Protestant authority questions while we wrestle with popes, bishops, and the Vatican? Listen to a certified Protestant scholar:

Five centuries after the Reformation the question of authority is still not settled for Protestants. Whereas Roman Catholics have the pope and the magisterium, and the Orthodox have Holy Tradition, most Protestants insist that they rely solely on Scripture, and that they either have no traditions or have traditions that are not on a par with Scripture. Some Protestants, however, would not only acknowledge a role for tradition but would also say that the Holy Spirit directly inspired Melanchton and Luther. How else could these two have taken upon themselves to redefine a sacrament, reduce the number of sacraments to two (or is it three?), delete books of Scripture, circumscribe communication with the saints and the mother of God and change the basis of theological decision from objective councils to subjective consciences? The nature of authority and the relation of tradition, Scripture and the Holy Spirit in Protestant churches remains a real, if often hidden, issue.[9]

To this I add the remarks of one of this generation's leading Protestant thinkers, William Stringfellow, who writes quite boldly in *Sojourners:*

> The weirdest corruption of contemporary American Protestantism is its virtual abandonment of the word of God in the Bible. That is ironic because access to the Bible and devotion to the Word of God was that out of which authentic Protestantism came into being. It is strange, too, because though the Bible suffers neglect in Protestantism, the Protestants continue to boast of their esteem for the Bible.

As for that fundamental Reformation doctrine of the priesthood of all the faithful, everywhere, it is safe to say, it is honored – has always been thus honored – more in name than in fact:

> Of all the new ideas, doctrines, and ministry practices that received scripts from the Reformation, one reform, the priesthood of all believers, has had much less impact on the church than might have been expected. For centuries, church people have talked, reflected, cogitated, preached, taught, and established committees and commissions to thrash out the meaning and practices inherent in the priesthood of all. But while Christians have thumbed their scripts until they are dog-eared, they haven't been given their cue to walk on the stage to play their part in the work of the church.[10]

There are other problems. One publication starts off an article on clergy divorce this way: "More clergy marriages are failing than ever before. In fact, clergy divorces are increasing in numbers at such an alarming rate that I believe this is the single most important issue the church must face if it is to stay authentic." News reports are relating that nationwide 50 percent of the Jews have no affiliation with a Jewish organization, forcing Orthodox, Conservative, and Reform synagogues to reach out to them with unconventional methods. Or, if you wish, consider some of these items from the sensitive book on Protestant clergy, *Pastors in Ministry:*[11]

1. The study shows that Lutheran clergy feel most positive and the most negative pretty much about the same things we do. On the positive side, beginning with the highest rating, are: preaching, worship leading, teaching of adults, visitation of the sick, ministry with the aged and counseling. On the negative side in descending order: youth work, evangelism, community responsibilities, administration, prophetic witness, confirmation and special group work (p. 19).

2. Most clergy need to be in control. A 1980 study on church growth said, "Pastors all too often do not feel confident nor productive in their work unless they are the central doers of ministry". . . . Is the need to control not only a factor in one's choice of ministries but also in a failure to stimulate lay leadership? (p. 27).

3. 40% of the clergy at least tended to agree that "I feel competitive pressure with brother and sister pastors to the point that it is difficult to be open and vulnerable" (p. 111).

4. Clergy have a strong sense of need for this lay participation but they apparently also need assistance in learning how to catalyze it. . . Clergy may also need assistance in dealing with the potential threat that increased lay participation may bring (p. 158).

5. The problem is not the demands of God but rather the unrealistic exceptions that we put on ourselves or that success orientated society puts on us (p. 91).

Finally, you might want to enjoy and relate to this unscientific poll which determined the five worst mistakes a pastor can make in the parish ministry. From the magazine *Lutheran Survey*, we find the results of a survey listing in order the highest number of responses: (1) failing to allow quality time for spouse and family, (2) solo performing, (3) forgetting names, especially at funerals and weddings!, (4) putting off preparation for preaching and teaching, and (5) "being either a ruthless ruminator or an uncommunicative communicator." There are other follow-up "dishonorable mentions," such as: unpolished shoes, tennis shorts at the hospital ICU, driving too fast, too much drinking, using sleazy stories, and coarse language.

All of us can both recognize and feel for our brothers and sisters in all of these issues. Our own problems from quantity to lay participation, then, are not unique. So many difficulties are simply endemic to the ministry, probably because, basically, the issues of ministry are the same everywhere, and the same types of personalities tend to ministry. No one has a corner either on all the virtues or all the vices, and maybe, in a perverse sort of way, to recognize that may put our own morale problems into perspective.

The sixth bit of good news is this: there will always be creative responses to our shortages and our needs. For example, in the Archdiocese of Denver in 1981, an ad hoc committee was formed to investigate alternate parish styles. What emerged was a model based on the small Christian communities like those in Africa and Latin America. In the particular example at hand, the Spirit of Peace parish in Denver, there is no pastor as such but rather a five member team and a priest-enabler who is pastor in another parish. The real innovation here is the covenant they made to share Protestant church facilities, thus for themselves eliminating costs, mortgages, drives, and maintenance.

As a result of sharing the facility, 80 percent of the Catholic funds can be used directly for ministry, not to mention providing a grass roots opportunity for ecumenism. The people meet in private homes every other week for two or three hours of prayer, Scripture listening and sharing, shared experiences, and sometimes they celebrate a paraliturgy, all of which is aided and directed by the team. [12] It's an interesting experiment worth watching. But for us here and now, the point is that out of need and necessity new forms are really emerging to respond. The Spirit is moving still. And that's good news.

There is also the story of Sacred Heart parish in Flint, Michigan, which faced a shutdown because there was no full-time priest available. A married couple has taken over as parish administrators. Bishop Povish said that closing the parish was his first choice, but that "this particular parish was doing some very fine outreach things, and they didn't want to quit. I didn't want to discourage them. . . . I think it's working."

Finally, we should take note once more of the survey findings that showed that 54 percent of adults and 74 percent of college campus students see restructuring parish leadership as a higher priority than recruiting new priests. "Clearly anyone studying the coming priest shortage needs to take seriously the strength of the viewpoint expressed here in Statement B [of the survey]—that, 'we must first of all think of new ways to structure parish leadership.' "[13] So maybe Kenneth Guentert is on to something when he writes, "Forget about the priest shortage. The term implies that the church will benefit from more priests. Frankly, I doubt it. More priests will mean more of the same priest- centered church we have now, and that's the last thing Catholics need."[14]

Our seventh (notice the mystical number) and final bit of good news is that in many places genuine attention is being given to priests. It may have taken a crisis to do it, but in some places it's happening. Among priests there are prayer groups, Vince Dwyer's program or Emmaus and the like. Social gatherings, encouraged sabbaticals, sensitivity to personal needs and pressures are the new hallmarks in some dioceses. Things are happening. Take heart, Father.

So, then, for your homework, reread this chapter at least once a week and parts of it for your daily meditation. Contemplate our seven proclamations of good news:

1. Shortages are relative to needs. With more help and restructuring, we should be able comfortably (and at times not so comfortably) to meet those needs.

2. There are potential solutions to our shortages, and we might promote some of them. We can be helped now if we have the will to do so.

3. Both as a profession and as a church we do in fact enjoy high esteem. People love us and what we stand for.

4. A look at our history is a good way to view our present crisis and the view offers hope. We've come back before with strength, energy, and pizzazz.

5. Our colleagues of other traditions are all struggling with many of the same issues. We are not alone, nor are we the clerical Cinderellas cringingly inferior to our carefree sisters.

6. There will always be creative experiments to let us know that possibilities always exist. (Something to do with the Spirit, I believe).

7. We're already in motion. The signs are good among us in many places, if only like a cloud, the size of a fist.

The good pastor decided that today he would finally get around to visit some of his parishioners, make some house calls. So he came to one house, knocked on the door, but no one answered. He had an instinct that somebody was in there, so he kept knocking louder and louder until finally a tiny voice from within the house said, "Come in, come in."

He tried the door and found it unlocked, so he stepped inside. He was in a little corridor and heard the voice again, "Come in, come in." He followed the sound down the hallway to a door, opened it, and entered a kitchen.

From inside the kitchen, he heard the voice again saying, "Come in, come in."

Just as the pastor looked around to find the owner of the voice, he suddenly found himself face to face with a huge ferocious, and growling German shepherd. The dog lunged at him and pinned him against the kitchen wall with his enormous paws on his shoulders breathing fire and brimstone.

At that moment, the pastor saw a parrot sitting in a cage over the kitchen sink saying, "Come in, come in."

"Oh, you stupid bird," cried the pastor, "don't you know any other words besides 'come in, come in'?"

"Yes I do," said the parrot. "Sic 'em, sic em!"

The pastor, it was said, was inaccessible on
weekdays and incomprehensible on weekends.

IV

The Image

WHEN IT COMES TO THE PRIESTLY SELF-IMAGE, WE RUN SMACK INTO
a glaring paradox. As we saw in the last chapter, both
organized religion in general, and the Catholic priest in particular, are held in high esteem, even at this very writing.
Priests, in Greeley's survey, "are at least as important in the
lives of the lay people as they used to be." But then he adds
the paradox we're talking about, "But unfortunately, perhaps
because of poor communication with lay people, they do not
seem to have as much confidence in the importance of their
own ministry as they had in the years before the Second
Vatican Council."[1]

Why is it, that while all the polls show the priest to be
as important as ever, priests themselves do not perceive it
that way? Why is morale so low and the priestly tendency
to self-pity so high? Why is his image so tarnished and blurred
in his own eyes? What happened at Vatican II and its aftermath to reduce the priest to such self-doubt, so much so that,
critically, very few are willing actively to recruit for their

53

replacement? Answers are very hard to come by, and data
are scarce, but we can venture a few guesses.

To begin with, there are those factors we've mentioned
already. Certainly all those resignations are shattering. Who
can feel good about a profession in which so many are quit-
ting, especially when the press (thanks a lot) says they're the
best and the brightest? Who's going to recruit for an outfit
whose members are leaving by the back door faster than you
can bring them in the front door? Less numbers, more work,
burnout, graying heads—who's able to look into the morning mirror and declare that all's right with the clerical world?

Then there's the identity problem, and I mean all around.
First, the identity of just being Catholic. What does it mean
in today's world? Bishop James Malone put it this way:

> A good deal of what I and others now see as needed in
> Catholic life in the United States can be subsumed under
> the heading of "Catholic identity." It will be apparent,
> I trust, that I am not speaking of Catholic chauvanism
> or Catholic triumphalism. I refer rather to a clear sense
> of what it means to be Catholic and also a healthy pride
> in membership in this spiritual community. Certainly
> a sense of Catholic identity is necessary among our
> young people, but it is also necessary in order to reinstill
> in Catholics generally a commitment to evangelization
> and a sense of mission.[2]

So the general Catholic populace is not sure of its identity,
and so it's confusing for us leaders to know who and what
we're leading, and that doesn't make us feel good or very
confident.

Identity crises are beginning to trouble religious women
too. At least some tensions are arising between them and the
greatly increasing numbers of lay women who are training
for ministry. What is happening is that the lay women are
now beginning to compete for those jobs formerly exclusively
held by religious women. And so, as their numbers decline
and lay women's numbers increase, religious women also
have to come to terms with their identity and special charisms.

Finally, there are the priests. "Who am I?" they ask, "and
what do I do for a living if everyone else is chipping away
at my traditional role?" Or, if you want a more philosophical
query:

> No group within the Catholic Church was more affected
> by this linguistic revolution [i.e., tampering with
> centuries-old sacred language] than the priesthood. For
> the priest was the linguistic practitioner par excellence,
> the guardian of the sacred language. His expertise was
> linguistically apparent and his role liguistically founded.
> It matters not how well or poorly he actually
> commanded the sacred language. To the ears of the pro-
> fane it could not but seem awesome. The simple yet
> complex act of turning this minister of the sacred toward
> the congregation and putting into his mouth words that
> were no longer archaic and arcane, but ordinary and all
> too human, effectively shattered a role and called into
> question an identity. Once the linguistic monopoly was
> ended, the query was bound to surface: what *does* the
> priest do that others cannot do? And with much embar-
> rassment many stammered for an answer.[3]

Well, it's all happened. The priest moans. "The liturgy committee has choreographed the Mass I used to prepare, lectors will do the readings I used to do, a deacon will proclaim
the gospel I used to proclaim, cantors will sing my songs,
eucharistic ministers will bring Communion to sick Mrs.
Smith, not I. The finance committee will challenge my request for new vestments, and the parish council will set the
agenda for the coming year." Such blurring of the traditional
priestly role naturally tends to confuse the priest's self-image.
And now, what's this the polls are telling him: that he is often
the *least* educated person among his parishioners? *"How long,
O Lord, how long!"* Father John Heagle sums up our cry with
delightful slyness:

> The pastor does not make decisions; he facilitates con-
> sensus. He does not mandate; he consults. He doesn't
> deliver a sermon; he shares a homily. And when the
> Parousia arrives, he will be at a meeting.

The former titles are no longer in vogue. The pastor is no longer referred to as the Dispenser of Sacraments, the Alter Christus, or the High Priest. He is now known as enabler of ministries, convener of community, facilitator of growth,and president of the assembly. He no longer saves souls; he impacts people.

In the seminary there was a saying that "the good ones always leave and the smart ones never come." That leaves the rest of us: clay vessels in the vineyard, shepherds without portfolio, sometimes courageous, often confused but still following the wind of the Spirit.[4]

So, (1) fellow priests leaving; (2) the laity armed with Bibles, documents, and degrees; (3) sisters, the best educated group in the whole world; (4) married deacons and married converted clergymen—they're shaking the priest's confidence. They're all taking a piece out of him until he fears he has nothing left. Moreover, as we've seen, the Big Three C's have let him down. The (5) Council wrote a lot about bishops and laity, but not about pastors; (6) the Revised Code did the same, and (7) the chancery, projecting the composite personality of its members, remains psychologically incapable of caring or affirming. So there you are, the mystical number again; seven reasons why no one should ask the priest why he's feeling so poorly about himself.

Still, there's got to be something deeper here. All those aforesaid reasons are valid but, I suspect, more so on the surface. There are wider issues here, what I call, for lack of a better term, contexts. There are, in fact, four of them that I believe powerfully affect the priestly image in a negative way.

The first is imagery and institution, the latter afflicting the former. That is, the reputation of the institutional church, either as perceived or actual, is bad news, and that bad news rubs off on us. The "Church" as the press puts it, comes across as arrogant, insensitive, unduly legal-minded, pharisaic, single-issued (sex, of course), persecutor of its prophets, and hostile to the very spirit of the gospel it professes to proclaim.

What was it that Father John Catoir, director of The Christophers, said to the Paulist Fathers on their 125th anniversary? "After nearly ten years as the chief judge of a diocesan marriage tribunal and five years as clergy personnel director during a period when 10,000 priests left the active ministry, and now nearly seven years as the director of The Christophers, after having traveled around this country giving talks and listening to people from all walks of life, I have come to believe that vast numbers of Catholics have distanced themselves from the church for a shocking reason: they perceive the church to be unforgiving. Of course, it is not true, but it is the impression they have of the church." Or, take this editorial comment from the English publication, *The Month:*

> A deep wound has been afflicted by a remote Curial department, not only on Father Boff himself [Latin American liberation theologian], but on all those priests and religious up and down Latin America who exhaust themselves and often risk their lives in making the Church of the Poor a living, vibrant reality. . . . The most worrying aspect of the Fr. Boff affair is that it seems to represent a denial of human rights.[5]

I choose this editorial because it is among the more moderate, and because it catches all the anti-institutional themes: remote Curial heavy-handedness, discouraging those in the field, opposing the gospel, perpetrating injustice. Others under public scrutiny by that "remote Curial department" have been Fox, Schillebeeckx, Curran, and McBrien. And who has forgotten those figures of the past, initially rapped, latter praised, such as Congar, Rahner, Chenu, Teilhard de Chardin, and deLubac?

The "heartless" institution continues to make local headlines in papers that specialize in them, like the *National Catholic Reporter:* "Archbishop expels pregnant schoolgirls, fathers," ran one such headline. And everyone cries out at the inhumanity of it all. Calling theologians on the carpet, denying ordination to women, censoring catechisms, insisting on the prohibition of birth control, removing professors, etc., are public policies, right or wrong, that give the accumulated image of a church that is authoritarian, political, and repressive to the extreme. And, again, that rubs off on the priest and stamps him with an image he does not want. And not only can't he shake it but he is further frustrated by his inability to reverse it. For example, have you ever noticed that when Father Jones is kind, considerate, helpful, and pastoral, it is Father Jones who is a nice guy. But, when Father Smith is rotten, unhelpful, legalistic, and authoritarian, it is the Church (yes, with a capital C) that is such.

So it comes down to this: all the nice things that an individual priest does are reduced to personal idiosyncrasies, while all the nasty things an individual priest does are inflated to the whole, universal Catholic Church. Our imagery is strictly Catch-22; the negative institutional image tarnishes our personal image, but the personal image does not brighten the church image. Anyway, there is no question that the Catholic church imagery is generally unfavorable, often unfairly so and with undisguised prejudice, but often accurately. Here's a letter, for example, appearing in *The Christian Century*, a liberal Protestant magazine. It comments on a previous article on abortion by Rosemary Radford Ruether:

> The crux of Rosemary Radford Ruether's article, "Catholics and Abortion: Authority vs. Dissent" (Oct. 2) is not really abortion. It is her very honest, fair, and accurate assessment of the Roman Catholic Church's hierarchy and its hopelessly anachronistic ways. Either the Roman Catholic Church is lost in another century or it fears talented people. Perhaps both.
>
> While other Christians are dealing with such vital matters as peace with justice, spiritual renewal and fair employment for female clergy, the Roman Catholic Church is speaking about papal infallability and a ban on contraception, and teaching justice while maintaining a system oppressive to women.
>
> On the other hand, as one notes in Dr. Ruether's article, the people who are being "blackballed" are very talented

folk: Daniel Maguire, Elizabeth Schussler, Hans Kung, etc. Why are they so feared?

As a former Roman Catholic turned United Church of Christ clergyperson, I watch this entire affair with a sense of amusement, but also with pain. I often wonder how such intelligent men could be so blind to justice, talent and creativity. My hunch is that the tightening of things, which seems to be Rome's approach prior to the November [1985] synod, will, along with the results of the synod, succeed in strangling an already choking church.

I can only say to those who dissent from the Roman Catholic Church: If you are censured and find you have become a *persona non grata*, please do not feel left out of "the church." We of the wider Christian church have our problems, but we will always welcome you as sisters and brothers in Christ. After all, it is Christ whom we serve, and not a hierarchy. Isn't it?[6]

Besides a certain blatant unfairness and, perhaps, more than a touch of the rejected suitor bias, nevertheless the letter captures a widely accepted image of the Catholic Church, especially among the intelligentsia. That there is a certain truth to the description is undeniable. But what is worse is that such a negative image discredits an enormous number of priests and religious who are doing incredible work with care, sensitivity, and heroism.

Is this the reason that one of the two major influences in recruiting vocations to the priesthood—priests personally asking (and the boys' mothers are the other)—is lacking? As the Greeley report says, "...the most serious obstacle to increasing the number of priestly vocations still seems to be the lack of encouragement which young men ought to receive from priests themselves."[7] Are some priests embarrassed to actively recruit for an organization that is known for its public image of repression, censorship, and authority? As the authors of *In Search of Excellence* quote, "People tune out if they feel they are failing, because the 'system' is to blame. They tune in when the system leads them to believe they are successful."[8]

Again, the tragic irony is that there are so many dedicated

priests, religious, and laity, but often they are generally acknowledged and admired only to the extent that they are seen as deviates from or prophets in (or against) the institutional church. Anyway, think of the people in all those Catholic caring facilities, in those schools doing incredible work with children, witnessing in the inner cities of the land. Surely, one of the priorities of our National Bishops' Conference must be to put aside funds to hire Madison Avenue to tell the world about these people, that they represent the best in the Catholic church. Somewhere in the land there has to be a public successor to Fulton Sheen. Somehow our corporate image must be made to approximate the gospel images of the Prodigal's Father, the Searching Shepherd, the Weeping Mother. There is a more human and compassionate version of the church than is currently discernable. Look, at the worldwide attraction for an old, fat pontiff who called the council; or the attraction of a Weston Priory, a Taize community, or a Jean Vanier's *L'Arche*. People, especially the young, are drawn to these warm places like bees to pollen.

We've got to turn around the institutional image if for no other reasons than to promote vocations and give us a sense of confidence. We need to be reassured in the knowledge that we work for a caring "company" where "People are our most important product." Again, as the authors of *In Search of Excellence* remark about certain large successful corporations, "Caring runs in the veins of the managers of these institutions. People are why those managers are there, and they know it and live it. The orientation is bone-deep and embedded in the language itself. At Delta, it's the "Family Feeling." At Hewlitt-Packard, it's "The HP Way".... Employees are called 'crew members' rather than personnel at McDonalds, 'hosts' at Disney Productions and 'associates' at J.C.Penny."[9]

It is noteworthy that we have no equivalent language in the church.

The second deeper context for our poor self image may lie in the words of Scripture. "I have this against thee: thou hast left thy first love." That is to say, we have allowed ourselves to be put upon with all kinds of extraneous tasks at the expense of our primary role of spiritual leadership — the most desired quality, as we shall see by both clergy and people — and have suffered a lost of focus as a result.

> What's keeping the young men from the seminaries isn't necessarily celibacy — it is a lack of image as to who and what a priest is, or why his vocation may be worthwhile in a world such as this with so many alternate attractions.
>
> "The priest's main job is still running the parish plant," a northern priest said. "You could as easily be running a hardware store or small business. Is that really what we are priests for?" The visiting is fine and important and sacramental, he said, but with so many other people in the parish doing the visiting and the ministries, the priest seems like one of the boys. Where they (the priests) really should be shining, standing out, as spiritual leaders to the flock, and in spite of what studies might show, the average priest hasn't got time.
>
> Those called to be priests are worn out by everyday chores before they can get to the spiritual duties that were the basis of their calling.[10]

This being spiritually "off center" may not only add to our confusion but muddy our image as well.

The third context that impinges on our self image is allied to the second; that is, we have inherited a one-sided spirituality that is out of sync with the Incarnation. This is to say that, deep down, most of us are practical Gnostics. Unlike biblical thinking our spirituality is rooted in Platonic other-worldliness. The world is not our home; we're just passing through. To be holy, therefore, is to be "apart," distant, remote, and above all, flawless, while straining to cast off this mortal coil and become purified spirits. In practical terms, we don't show our human side. We repress. And we repress not just because we're like the average American male who does that all the time, but also because we're priests, men of God, who have our feelings under control.

But of course, we don't. Still, against the grain, we strive unconsciously to give the appearance of being sanctimonious and inhuman. So when the media, which are fairly prejudiced anyway, depict the priest they can only come up with Spencer Tracy's Father Flannagan, Bing Crosby's Father O'Malley, or the insipid Father Mulcahey of M*A*S*H. Only Robert Blake of TV's *Hell Town*, which became a casualty in the competition rating game, gave us a Father Noah "Hardstep" Rivers who showed some human passion. His portrayal may not have been to everyone's liking—he was quick with his fists and quicker with his tongue—but he struggled with the human condition and injustice and let his feelings show. And if at times he went too far, at least he was coming across as a member of the human race.

Could it be that our image is paradoxically tarnished with too much tinsel? That both for ourselves and others our image is under suspicion and strain because of unrealistic role models? (I think of the story of St. Aloysius who, it is said, closed his eyes when nursing as an infant at his mother's breasts!) Caught between Bing Crosby and Robert Blake, we are conditioned to play the former and suppress the latter and so effectively deny both the incarnation and a compelling, human, priestly image.

The fourth and final context that undermines our clerical image is that most of us have simply failed to grasp an alternate identity. I mean that we suffer so much from everyone else taking over our job because we have ill-conceived what that job is. If we have continued to perceive ourselves as the priest who alone rules over the people, the one and only (remote) father who feeds them, the one in charge of the little flock, the one with the power to "confect" the sacraments, the one who alone has received the Spirit and has been officially designated through ordination to pass it on to others, then as these things disappear, we will indeed have an identity crisis, a battered and tattered image.

So these are our four wider "contexts" within which our imagery is constrained and emasculated. We've suggested a response to the institutional fallout, and we will discuss priestly spirituality in a later chapter. So now we must get ready in the next chapter—somewhat heavier than the others—to try to correct our self-understanding and, in the process, I hope, firmly and gloriously position ourselves in a recovered traditional imagery and identity.

Meanwhile, as we ponder these four reasons why our image is poor, we might also come to see why we have so few vocations. The psychological truism is that images correspond to deep human yearnings and needs, and the more appealing the image the more the pursuit of it. The images presented to the young are enhanced considerably by the stories of successful people who tell of their peak moments and challenges and excitement, people who are glad to talk to them about the work they obviously enjoy. As priest psychiatrist James Gill points out, however, when it comes to priests, their work life is considerably less excitingly described. Alas, considerably less.

The attitude that comes across most often is not excitement but long suffering! Very few priests talk about their peak moments or the joy or the challenge. Young people catch a distant glimpse of our lives as routine, boring, and unspectacular. They have no idea of our camaraderie, our vacations, our intellectual growth, our spiritual battles, our professional skills. They have no notion of how we celebrate each other's birthdays, jubilees and anniversaries, how we sing, create, or ply our hobbies. They don't know our friendships and quiet devotions and heroisms and, most of all, our relationship to God. They never hear what a kick we get out of celebrating liturgy, the thrill of baptizing and holding an infant in one's arms, working with engaged couples, being confident to so many. They don't know what peace comes from reconciling a long-time stray or touching the sick with holy oil and peace. They don't sense how we feel the people's love and admiration and acceptance and what a deep happiness and support that is.[11]

Why don't they know these things? Because no one tells them! Because we have a false modesty. Because we're intimidated by the media, which give them plastic larger-than-life heroes. Because we're unsure of ourselves. Because, unfortunately, we may believe our own poor self-image. Because some of us are so busy gazing at our clerical navels we've missed the joy and have squandered the time on ourselves that we ought to be sharing with others.

We're like Uriah Heep or Charlie Brown instead of like Zorba. Certainly we don't have to be like the Pepsi ads jumping high at the volleyball net in a flash of soda-induced ecstasy (although it couldn't hurt!). But that confused, long-suffering image has got to go if we're to attract the young people. I think it was Plato who said that the one who controls the images controls society. The "children of darkness" surely understand that better than the children of the light. We don't all have to run out and get our teeth capped or a TV hairpiece, but we do have to share what is really true about ourselves deep down: that we do have wonderful moments, that it is awesome (both colloquially and theologically) to deal so intimately with the mysteries of faith and be such a precious part of people's lives. As someone said, "Funny, you don't look saved." If we don't, we won't attract others. The image needs refurbishing.

Anyway, if you can make the proper adjustments, you can resonate with this story in the light of what has been said so far:

> One day, Arnie, my husband, pointed out to me that every word I said sounded exactly like my mother. So he sent me into analysis, and I worked on it for a year. But when I thought I sounded better, Arnie, my husband, point out to me that every word I said sounded exactly like my father. So he sent me back to analysis and I worked on it for a year. But when I thought I sounded better, Arnie pointed out that every word I said sounded like my analyst. So he had me change analysts, and I worked on it for a year. Now it is over six months and every word I say sounds like my husband. He thinks I'm cured!

Lovely Lady, dressed in green,
Make me preach like Bishop Sheen.

V

The Likeness

THE HEART AND SOUL OF WHO AND WHAT WE ARE, OUR CLEAREST, sharpest, and most authentic image, is summed up in the word "leadership." We must recall that Jesus picked out disciples to whom were given the ability to understand the mysteries. Christianity's earliest New Testament writing, the Epistle to the Thessalonians (around the year 50), clearly testifies to its local leaders, "those among you who are over you [literally, "those who stand before you"] in the Lord and admonish you," whom Paul charges the Thessalonians to respect and esteem (5:12-13). Clement of Rome (A.D.91) distinguished between laity and clergy (though not with the sharpness of passive-active that came in the early and later Middle Ages). And so it goes: leadership was always a necessary part of the church simply because the church was also a human community. The presbyter-priest, of whom we are the descendants, had his origin in such leadership, first as local leaders, advisors to the bishop; and, later, as his delegate at far-flung, country communities ("parish priest"). But note: such leadership was not conceived as funneling the

Spirit of a Spiritless people, but as evoking and gathering that
already community Spirit in prayer, worship, and service.

Notice, also, the New Testament assumption that ministry
was rooted firmly within the matrix of community. The emphasis was on the Spirit and the charismatic, as opposed to the
paternal and the institutional.therefore, the whole Christian
community, so endowed with the Spirit, becomes the corporate
reference point for any ministry. In a word, all ministry, including that of the priest, finds its proper setting within the
whole people of God. Therefore, it is with some significance
that the earliest ordination rite we have from the Apostolic
Tradition, around the year 215, has the emphasis on governance,
not on the eucharist. In this rite, there was no sense of a communication of power, but rather a being brought into the order
of presbyters, who formed the council for the bishops.

I need not detail what happened in subsequent centuries:
how the concept of the whole community being ministerial slowly but surely contracted until the community was emptied
of its charisms, which were transferred to the priest alone.
Unique ordination rather than democratic baptism became
the source of grace, ministry, and the touchstone with God,
so much so that most of us grew up with a theology which
justified that. You can sense this change in the fourth-century
ordination prayers. Two hundred years after the Apostolic
Tradition, no longer were such prayers for wisdom and
counsel but for the dignity of the presbyter. Sacredness was
now applied to the presbyter since he was now doing sacred
things. And the prayer for the deacon was that he may ad-
vance to a higher order!

In our day, quite disturbingly for many, a dramatic return
has been made – and it is a return – to the original design, and
we've been caught off guard. Ministry is once more seen as
rooted in the community as a whole, rather than in the individual priest in whose ministry some people are allowed
to share. In our time, the clue to this dramatic change came
when the church once more began ordaining married
deacons. The message was that ministry was indeed capable

of being exercised by married believers. It was, finally and officially, Pope Paul VI in his *motu proprio, Ministeria Quaedam* who finally broke the clerical monopoly of ministry and returned it to the people. So, once more then, the Spirit becomes the whole reference point for any reflection on ministry. All ministry, including that of the priest, finds its proper setting within the community, with the calling of the whole people of God. Within this community, the priest is now being asked to make his own Moses' words: "I wish that all the Lord's people were prophets and that the Lord would confer his Spirit on them all!" (*Numbers* 11:29) – not an easy statement for men used to dealing with power.

Yet, it might be accurate to say that this whole cataclysmic shift affects our age old leadership role, not so much in its definition as in its style. As Robert Imbelli says, "The one who is ordained to the priesthood within this community of the Spirit is ordered to the building up of *this* community. His leadership, then, is specified by the nature of the community from which he is called and to whose service he is consecrated."[1] In other words, we are intimately connected with community leadership, but that leadership is not that of solo dictator, but more of a father, a gatherer, an enabler, a focus of the community's symbols, a celebrant of the already Spirit present in the whole people of God. As Peter Fink puts it – and you have to read his words carefully:

> There is no hint in the *lex orandi* that the Spirit is given to the ordained in order that they in turn may pass it on to others. That is an unfortunate image drawn once the church is funneled into priest and bishop, and once the personal presence of God becomes imaged as an entity to be doled out in different amounts. In that image set, one can only give what one has received. If the *lex orandi* is given a proper hearing, it becomes clear that the reason why the ordained person goes forth to invoke God's Spirit upon others is the very reason the Spirit was invoked upon him. It belongs to the structure of the church's prayer to invoke God's Spirit whenever a tranformation is sought or when a mission is seen which can

only be fulfilled with God's help. And within that structure is the ministry of the ordained to lead, and thus pray, the prayer of the church. The Spirit of God resides in the church, manifests itself in the activities of the church, and is in fact constitutive of the church. Since the liturgy is the activity of the entire church, the power of God's Spirit in the church is the only power that can be invoked and made manifest.

The ordained are assigned ministries within the prayer and activity of the church, and as such their role is primarily one of service. It is a service, certainly, to the people of the church. Most profoundly, however, it is a service to the abiding presence of God-Spirit whose power is activated and made manifest when the ordained conduct their assigned ministries. The ordained are thus ministers of this power, not because they possess it in any special way, but because they are commissioned and authorized by the church to perform the very actions which manifest and contain that power. The heart of this image shift is the realization that the ordained in their ministry are placed at the disposal of God's Spirit. It is not the other way around.[2]

Furthermore, it is important to recall that the church is always becoming. It is rooted and nourished in the past ("Do this in remembrance of me."), and it strives to become what it is called to be in the future. We both remember the past and are summoned to the future, and it is in the guided resolution of these two tensions that presbyteral or priestly leadership has its foundation. As community leaders we assemble the people (the church gathered) from their everyday witnessing lives (the church scattered), and , in the eucharistic prayer, over which we preside (derived substantially from our community leadership), we invoke the common past and promised future that shape the people of God.

It is this very "largeness" of our task, as Peter Fink calls it, that makes it necessary for the presbyter-priest to be ordained by the college of bishops, and not through the local ministry of the church; much the same way as that Thessalonian community is envisaged by Paul not as a self-contained

group, even though they have local leaders, but as in active
contact with "all believers in Macedonia and Achaia" (1:7 and
4:10) and "the churches of God in Christ Jesus which are in
Judea" (3:2).

> What the sacrament of order then does is to give the
> recipient a new role in the life of the church, and, as
> principal expression of this, a special role in the celebra-
> tion of the eucharist, where the mystery of the church
> is celebrated. His position becomes such that in the
> celebration of the Lord's Supper, the relationship to
> Christ as founder and source of life, as well as the rela-
> tionship to the community of the apostles and to the
> communion of all the churches, is expressed and serv-
> ed through his presidency. Because he is empowered to
> represent the church in this vital action, to represent to
> it its own very ground of being, we say that he is em-
> powered to represent Christ.[4]

Perhaps a couple of clergymen from another tradition
have put it all more simply for us when they observed, "It
is not that other people could not pray, preach, teach, heal
and administer the sacraments as well or better than the
priest, it is that, when the priest does these things, he or she
functions as the symbol-bearer of the community, as the officially recognized, corporately designated person to bear and
interpret the community's shared symbols. And that makes
all the difference."[5] We are indeed, as Karl Rahner said, a kind
of living sacrament of Jesus gathering and in gathering effectively preserving the people both from amnesia (forgetting
their roots) and nostalgia (forfeiting the future). And all this
is a magnificent calling, a profound and satisfying kind of
leadership.

These theoretical thoughts have very practical consequences
for our present malaise. If as leader I do not funnel the Spirit,
then I can share in evoking it. If I do not invent or confect
the sacraments I can mutually and cooperatively celebrate
them with the people of God. If I do not have all power, I
can recognize it where it exists in others (Mark 9:39). If I am
not sole practitioner of all ecclesiastical matters whatsoever,

I can be opened to shared and collaborative ministry. If I am not the power broker, I can be the servant broker. So, I don't have to be alarmed if there are lectors and cantors and eucharistic ministers. My leadership task is to bring "holy order" to such a mutual celebration, to orchestrate the liturgy, to lead the community's active worship. My service is to the community, so that it may be an authentic people of God. I don't have to fret about parish councils (existing, not how they work), because together we are the church or parish. It is the people's, and I am a significant and necessary steward of that reality. My genuine leadership is not one of autonomous power and imposition, but one of service and enablement.

You see, it's a matter of perception. If I perceive myself as overlord of the parish plant, as general manager with full unilateral power, the ordained guru – then, indeed, I will be dismayed and distraught over the various encroachments of my power and position and will likely retreat into stiff and unyielding authority for preservation and protection. But if I perceive myself as a genuine presbyter-leader, whose ordained and certain leadership consists not in parceling out divine power, but rather in calling forth the power of the resident community Spirit, in gathering the people, in co-celebrating the mysteries with them ("The ancients... habitually spoke of 'doing the Eucharist,' 'performing the mysteries,' 'making the synaxis' and 'doing the oblation'... used all their active language about 'doing' the liturgy quite indifferently of laity and clergy alike" – Dom Gregory Dix[6]) and collaborating with them in the mission of the church, then I need not fear an active church, a variety of gifts, or even the prophets who, always breaking through existing stuctures, are a pain in the neck to us all. In brief, once I set my sights on the fact that I am not the church, but we are, that the whole church has been given the mission of Christ, that the whole church is basically ministerial, then I can find it easier (at least with some encouragement and retraining) to move into a style of leadership that appreciates these facts.

So I guess we're saying that we have to reposition ourselves. We, who historically began as community leaders and official foot-washers for the right ordering of community and wound up as exclusive holders of personal power, must backtrack and re-focus ourselves in relationship to the people of God. We need less emphasis on some ontological power to confect the eucharistic body of Christ, as Pope John Paul II reminded us in his Holy Thursday sermon in 1984, and more emphasis on "confecting" the community body of Christ. It takes leadership to make it all work, to pull together a wide variety of ministries. It's just that, within this variety, we have to remember that the charism of priestly leadership is one of them, not all of them. As John Coleman reminds us, "Every ministry in the Church is a limited gift and service within the wider body containing a rich variety of ministerial gifts."[7]

So the ordained and the nonordained (there is always something unnerving about describing others in the negative) are complementary, not competitive. Still, it is important to remember and to proclaim loudly in these days of priestly self-doubt Peter Chirco's observation that *whatever* the variety and scope of ministry, and however ministries come and go, "one ministry must always exist no matter what the circumstances of time and place. This is the overseeing ministry, the ministry of leadership of the whole people of God in the process of becoming more deeply a Christian community . . . (the ministerial priesthoood) is a unifying ministry. It coordinates, facilitates, gives common direction and purpose to all other ministries and to the actions of the faithful.[8] It is in this spirit that Archbishop Daniel Pilarczyk of Cincinnati remarks:

> We are going to need to continue to treasure and develop our priests. The present situation does not downplay the importance of priests, but increases it. Where there are many ministries, where people are more involved than ever before, the need of saintly, skilled, informed priestly leadership is greater than before. Priests will continue

to be needed for real priestly work, for the work of building up the Christian community around its eucharistic Lord. The priest is the consecrated leader, and the fact that there is more going on will mean that we need leadership more not less.[9]

Words like these are why I like Avery Dulles's definition of ordination as "a recognition of the gifts of leadership, and at the same time, a sacramental commissioning that empowers them to govern the community in the name of Christ." I also like his more recent addition to his famous models of the church: the church as "a community of disciples." Likewise I think Dolores Lecky is also on target when she describes the church as "a community of ministers," and, in this community of disciples, this community of ministers, we are the leaders.

Two homely images come to mind here that may be helpful. One is that of a mother who often functions symbolically and actually as a telephone operator. She connects all the distant grown up children with one another and is the focal point for cross-communications. She's the oil that keeps it all going, the dependable one for relaying messages, needs and hurts to be soothed, and the whereabouts of all. In short, she is cohesion for the family community and when she or dad dies that community tends to drift and re-form in other groups. The ordained priest is like that in that adult or grownup family we call the local parish community. In this community of disciples he gathers, symbolizes, and connects. The other imagery comes from an old sermon by Msgr. Ronald Knox who, trying to get us to see how our relationships is to God, likened that relationship to a dog and its master. The dog runs and roots and sniffs and picks up a stone or stick—but he constantly runs back to his master as a reference point. The dog's found stick is not nearly as exciting if he has no master to show it to and relate with him and who makes his discovery worthwhile. We are like the master.

Everyone, whether an individual or a community, needs a reference point to make it all worthwhile. We are that reference point and more.

Again, we are a critical sign in the lives of those so involved. We are reference, cohesion, and connector precisely because we are the official keeper of the community's traditional symbols of book, bread, ritual, and the ancient stories:

> In their search for excellence, Peters and Waterman found that it was generally people, rather than philosophies, structures, or incentives, that were the key. . . . People looked for two critical things from the setting in which they found themselves: first, and more important, meaning; and second, purpose and values. . . . If the needs for meaning, vision, purpose, mission, and values are so central to the corporation in pursuit of the healthy bottom line, how much more important must they be to those of us in pursuit of the reclamation and transcendence of our world? And consequently, in our own leadership behavior, how much of our time and attention is given to these questions? . . . The leader as "high priest," by means of articulation, socialization, and the development of reinforcing stories, myths and symbols, promotes a sense of organizational uniqueness and identification that renders excellence reachable and makes the excellence of the organization a source of meaning for its constituency.[10]

St. Mark's Episcopal parish in Washington is an unusual one of high charism and witness. The people there allowed their minister to take a six months' sabbatical with his family while they, the people, ran the church community. It was a fruitful and interesting experiment, forcing the people to be the church they claimed to be, but not without some stress and questions. The following commentary is significant:

> With their minister gone, St. Mark's people began to discover that in spite of their new-found power and responsibility, the idea of a "lay church" was a myth. A parson is a person with a difference. The nature of parish

life seemed to reject a vacuum at its center, and the people made efforts to fill it in various ways. Verna Dozier
feels that while the rector was physcially absent for six
months, actually there was no leadership vacuum: "they
were holding the parish together for Jim." John Terry,
and other parishoners, found Verna the temporary
center of the congregation's life, and she was deeply conscious of this role. Other members turned to the
seminarian, or to the parish secretary as a substitute rector. All these ways of acting out the need for a central
figure dramatized the senior warden's thoughtful comment: "It seems to me that the church as an organization needs at its center someone whose organizational
center is the church."[11]

All of us should read this particular witness many times. We
are leaders who count. We are critically significant. We are
the center. Our style may have to change, but our position,
sacramentalized beyond baptism in a long, ancient tradition,
is firm and true and needed. As Thomas O'Meara expresses
it, 'The capacity for leadership within a community of adults
is central to any theology and identity of the priest"—and that's
what we've tried to explore in this chapter.

Perhaps what makes us a bit nervous when we talk this
way about leadership is that the very concept implies power;
and power, in today's charged atmosphere of shared ministry,
feminism, and collegiality, is suspect. Any kind of power.
Nevertheless, it is an illusion—and a dangerous one—to think
that power is not an integral part of any community, much
less that it is not a part of the church community. The question is, as we have tried to show, not one of power, but what
kind of power and how it is used and shared. So, we must
openly admit and become comfortable with the reality that
in church theology, ordination bestows power not everyone
has. We have difficulty with the idea because many priests,
smarting from publicized abuses or new pressures, are reluctant to admit either that ordination gives them power or that
this power does in fact set them apart—especially the latter,
because this "setting apart" aspect of power seems to imply

moral superiority and who in democratic America wants to
be "holier than thou"?

Still, to deny the power and the apartness of ordination
leadership is ultimately to act irresponsibly and become prey
to a subversive false humility. We *are* morally different for
being ordained ministers. We are invited to enter into the lives
of people with an intimacy that few others share. We are
asked to exercise certain responsibilities for a community,
which cannot but help make us different. The priest who visits
a family that has had a death is there not just as another friend
or neighbor, but as the pastor, the one who represents the
church and therefore is God's presence, no matter how hesi-
tant or inadequate he may feel. The fact is, "Ordination results
in the modification of individuality. The gift of God's Holy
Spirit in the act of ordination alters the self as self and results
in the powerful reality of the self as representative figure."[19]
After you digest that, take time to read carefully these words
from Methodist moral theologian, Stanley Hauerwas, writing
in the Lutheran magazine, *Word and World* (Spring 1986).
Keep in mind that you're reading the words from a Protestant source.

> Part of our current difficulty is the failure by laity and
> minister alike to appreciate that those who have been
> called to the ministry are, or at least should be, made
> different by that calling. Put simply, ordination bestows
> on ministers the power not all in the church possess—
> e.g., they alone can preside at the eucharist. To possess
> such power requires them to have the [moral] character
> sufficient to that task as well as to protect them and the
> church from abuse of that power.

> I am aware that such language may sound far too
> "Catholic" for Protestant ears, but I think it is not only
> theologically justified but also more nearly does justice
> to the empirical realities of the ministry. For if the par-
> ticular character of the ministry is not acknowledged,
> the character of the office as well as those occupying
> it becomes far too subject to the cultural sentimentalities
> that currently sustain the assumption that"religion is a

good thing." Moreover, it is important that the question
of ministerial office and character be put in terms of
power, for it is not any specifiable knowledge or skill
that makes the ministry, though certainly knowledge
and skill will hopefully be present, but rather the power
the minister has been given to perform the rites of the
church for the church. For as most ordination rites make
clear, "all the baptised share the gifts of the Spirit, the
command to evangelize, witness, heal and serve." The
ministry, therefore, requires no skills or gifts that are
not generally available to anyone in the church. Rather
ordination is but the way "some Christians are designated
for the task of equipping the saints, caring for the church,
building up the community, representating the church
as a whole. In ordination the church puts some of its
folk under orders; it makes them official community people." In short, it gives them power (p. 183-184).

It is only abuse and intimidation that makes us associate
power with Citizen Kane. There's another model of real
power: Jesus Christ. It is only a crisis of ministerial self-
confidence that makes us yearn to be only "one of the guys."
It is only the confusion of the times that makes us feel that
there's no ground between the exercise of absolute raw power
and the acceptance of the lowest common denominator. It
is only a loss of identity that hides or denies the charism of
ordination's leadership power or the incisive force of its
symbolism.

As we end, permit me a short summary. In 1985, the arch-
diocesan newspaper of Oklahoma City candidly reported the
results of a priest questionnaire. The report surfaced the
following anxieties: First of all, not unexpectedly, priests
report being lonely. Secondly, they feel a distinct tension in
trying to empower the laity while really not knowing what
lay ministry is to begin with, what qualifications such people should have, and most of all, how to relate to the laity.
This last issue is not just a question of "getting along," but the
deeper one of identity. Sooner or later, the priests said, with
all that help from the lay people, what would be left for them

to do? As one of their spokesman asked, "What are we being freed for?"

That's a plaintive cry we've heard all through this book, and we've tried to respond to it in this chapter. Here, however, let me make a few more specific points. First of all, the question itself is sincere, but perhaps the wrong one to ask initially. The question "What are we being freed for?" carries all of the negative burden of the typical American image of success: I must *do* something. Success and affirmation come from doing. Therefore, if others do what I used to do, that leaves me empty and without identity, without a job description; and in America that is tantamount to social annihilation. The right question to be asked first is, I suggest, "What are we being freed to *be?* We are being freed to be that symbol which we described above. I know that being a symbol elicits no big thrill and makes us ask, "So, okay, I'm a symbol. What'll I do all day: just sit around like some icon to be trotted out for ceremonies?"

Hardly. Being a symbol is truly powerful. Every society, however primitive or sophisticated, needs a symbolic person who performs a most valuable function. The symbolic person is that "significant other" of psychological jargon who makes life and activity all worthwhile. Even a brilliant and involved laity needs a symbolic figure to make their jobs, in or out of the sanctuary, meaningful and affirmed. We are being freed to be a more authentic symbol for our people.

Next, we can say that we are being freed to concentrate on other neglected essentials such as (a) prayer, (b) study, (c) preparing homilies – our one big impressive moment to our largest audience, (d) providing support, encouragement, and connection, and (e) celebrating well. As we shall see later, time simply must be taken – much more time than our guilt now allows us – for prayer and study in particular (the others fall out easily from these two). Not needed for so much of the groundskeeping and administrative tasks, we are burdened with now; we can take the necessary time to get first things first in our own lives and hearts, in order to be something more for others.

Finally, let's not abandon common sense. "What are we being freed for?" It will be nigh on to the Parousia before we get a perfect laity using all their gifts and fulfilling every ministry: not even our Protestant counterparts have achieved that, as we have seen. I don't think we have to fear in the next thousand years or so of having nothing left to do in the everyday community life of our parish and its needs. We will continue to be needed, continue to have a job, continue to wonder if we'll ever have enough time. From my own experience I have found that, as in so many similar situations (like adding a new room and saying, how did I ever live in such small quarters and finding you need more room) that the more lay participation and collaboration you have, somehow or other, the more you have to do.

So, what's the bottom line? It is to wax philosophical and to soliloquize as follows: All right, our numbers are down and declining, but this presses us to more collaboration, such as the first Christians knew. Our recent identities are splintered as others pick up (reclaim?) the pieces. But this is good, for it forces us back to our original genius of presbyter-priest-enabler in whom perfection is both unnecessary and undesirable but in whom charity is essential. Okay, so marriage is on an equal footing with celibacy and we are no longer superior but different, but this opens us to explore our gift more radically and to ponder anew Pope John Paul II's words, "The priest, by renouncing the fatherhood proper to married men, seeks another fatherhood and, as it were, even another motherhood, recalling the words of the apostle about children whom he begets in suffering. . . . The heart of the priest, in order that it may be available for this service, must be free. Celibacy is a sign of a freedom that exists for the sake of service." Perhaps, a hint of what that freedom may mean for us may be found in the voluntary celibacy of the laypeople in the ecumenical community of Tazie or Jean Vanier's *L'Arche.* Our need to be needed has been shaken and scattered, but this too forces us to rediscover our *primary* need: not to be "all things to all men," burdened with unrealistic expectations as that Pauline phrase has become, but with the sense of responding freely, *within the context of mutual ministries* to the needs, joys, and hurts of the people of God. Or to put it more elegantly and scripturally:

> As servants of God we commend ourselves in every way: . . . genuine, yet regarded as imposters; known, yet regarded as unknown; dying, and yet we live on; beaten, and yet not killed; sorrowful, yet always rejoicing; poor, yet making many rich; having nothing, yet possessing everything. *(2 Cor. 6:3-10)*

I am suggesting that when we clean up the public image of the institutional church so that we have more of an upbeat company or, in less secular and more biblical language, a compassionate church; and when we return sincerely to our founding charism of community leadership with its accent on enabling service, then we will know who we are and what we are. When that happens, they will seek us out.

In our next chapter, we have to explore leadership and authority and collaboration in a bit more detail; meanwhile, after this heavy chapter, a few light stories are in order.

When the Pope visited Ireland it was, to be sure, a fine occasion for many a reconciliation and confession. Mike, being from a small island off the coast, didn't get to the mainland often and consequently not to confession often. However, he happened to be there at the time of the papal visit and, with so many others in the spirit of the event, went to confession. The priest urged him to go to confession more often, but Mike pleaded his remoteness on the island. But the priest persisted, reminding Mike that they now have those little planes what shuttle back and forth weekly, so there was no longer an excuse. "So," queried the priest, "how about the airplane, Mike?" Mike responded, "Nope. Too expensive for venial sins and too risky for mortal ones!"

Then there was the seminary history professor who was on his deathbed. Had he actually died yet? "Feel his feet," a seminarian on watch suggested. "No one ever died with warm feet." The professor opened his eyes and said, "Joan of Arc did," and died. (Joe Gallagher)

Finally—the pastor and his associate interrupted their annual trip to the football game to go to a dentist. Monsignor said,"I want a tooth pulled, and I don't want gas because I'm in a big hurry. So just extract the tooth as quickly as possible and we'll be on our way." The dentist was quite impressed and said, "You're certainly a courageous man. Which tooth is it?" The Monsignor turned to his associate and said, "Show him your tooth, Father!"

*The man rang the rectory bell. Father opened the
door. The man tried to speak and then had a
coughing fit. "I can't understand you." said Father
Smith. The man coughed and tried to speak again
but couldn't. "Wait,' said Father and went to the
kitchen and brought back a glass of water. "Drink
this," he said. "Now, how does that feel?" "Much
better," said the man in a clear voice. "Well," said
Father kindly, "what is it you wanted to say?"
"This is a stickup!"*

VI

Authority
and Leadership

In his address on May 17, 1985, to the workers in Antwerp,
Belgium, Pope John Paul II remarked, taking his cue from
Lumen Gentium (31 & 33): "Moreover, since the council, you
have become very conscious of this calling [to sanctify the
world], and I rejoice at that. It is not a matter of a present
concession on the part of pastors, who have greater need of
you because of their smaller numbers or because of the gravity
of the problems. You have a share in the church's mission
of salvation. You are called to the apostolate through your
baptism and your confirmation."

81

Note the Pope's acceptance of the shift: laity are part of the church's mission not, as in the old days "by participating in the work of the hierarchy," but by baptismal right. And, of course, this brings to surface over and over again the continuing tension, which, stated crudely, is where do we begin and they leave off? What's the difference between us and them: all those laity doing what we did formerly as part of their baptism-confirmation? As Scotty MacDonald, executive director of the U.S. Bishops' committee on priestly life, summed it up, "When much of what was strictly understood as 'priestly ministry' can be accomplished by others in the church, then the solid age-old identity of the priest shows a few cracks and has become a reason for discontent on the part of many priests." The official U.S. Report on the church since Vatican II says the same thing: "Although the emergence of new ministries and the involvement of large numbers of lay persons constitute one of the important developments in the Catholic church in the United States during the post conciliar period, this development has at times contributed to a blurring of the roles of the ordained and the non-ordained."

Well, we have tried to come to terms with this in the last chapter, stressing that our role is that of community leader with the emphasis on service and enablement and collaboration. Here, in the first part of this chapter, I want to define and clarify further the place of collaboration in our ministry and the things that tend to undermine its genuine place in the life of the church. Hopefully, we will also learn to define our leadership role better as well. I am borrowing here (and modifying somewhat) Sandra Schneiders's perceptive comments on the dilemmas and tensions of collaboration as it tries to take hold in our present structure.

The whole issue of collaboration started with Vatican II. That council went back and recovered an ancient description of the church as the people of God—a phrase that is culled from one of the church's earliest sense of itself as a continuation of and replacement for the chosen people of the Hebrew Scriptures. ("Those who belong to Christ are Abraham's offspring, heirs according to the promise."*/Galatians 3:29/.* The phrase implies that all the people are equally chosen, that there is a common ministry and witness for all. True, the council came down heavily reaffirming the hierarchial structure of the church; yet, at the same time, without attempting a reconciliation, spoke deliberately, emphatically, and affirmingly of the equality of all of God's people. The phrase people of God, in this sense and in our recent post-Tridentine context, is revolutionary. It implies a distinct restructuring of the church, at least in its relationship with those of the hierarchy (including pastors.)

If you unpack the phrase, says Schneiders, you come up with at least three concepts: (1) dialogue, (2) collegiality, and (3) collaboration. As for the first, dialogue, it tends to have a one-sided slant in our recent ecclesiastical history. It carries distinct overtones of talking nice to Protestants in order to win them over to the truth. Actually, of course, the word itself assumes equal partners, each of whom has something valid to say. Dialogue is not monologue. So as pastors we give no concession, to use John Paul's phrase, in speaking with the laity as a people of God. Rather, we must assume a stance of respect because our fellow church members have something to say. Dialogue does not preempt leadership, but enhances it. As we shall say frequently, it's a matter of style as well as of principle. There must be a give and take if we are serious about the phrase people of God. Arguments and discussion are accepted or rejected on the basis of their innate validity, not on the position of the debaters. If you want a little conscience pricking, you might meditate on the gospel instance where the "laity" was dismissed by the "hierarchy" on the basis of unilateral position, not on the cogency of the argument. So, look at John, Chapter 9, where we have the case of the man born blind who was healed on the Sabbath. When he argued with some force that God would hardly back up a healing sinner, he was summarily cut off with a stern reminder of status: "You were wholly born in sin, and you mean to teach us?"(34).

The second word "collegialtiy" has the word college in it and thereby implies equal participants whose contribution again is judged by the validity of word or work and not by the office of the speakers. (Here we might want to be a mouse in the room where Innocent I and the layman John Bernardone are conversing.) Finally, the word collaboration speaks in its etymology of people who literally co-labor at a common task. When you examine these three words as implicit in the phrase people of God and position them alongside the words hierarchy and leadership you find no necessary diminishing of either side. Rather, you sense an approach, a style, a certain way of seeing us all as church.

Actually, collaboration in the sense of these three words, in the sense even of authority is not the product of some new social theory or the peculiar product of our American way of life. We find roots for dialogue, collegiality, and collaboration in the New Testament itself. Jesus was openly dialogic, openly equalitarian. Certainly this is evident in his associates: Pharisees, tax collectors, fishermen, women, zealots, and even those who were not Jewish. In the tradition that first came down to us, no one was to lord it over another or assume the title of teacher. The poor and the rich, the saints and the sinners, were to eat at the same table. Men and women – really radical for the times – were to be baptized into the community and, what's more, even Gentiles and Samaritans were welcome. Slaves were to be received as brothers and sisters. Moreover, Jesus always seemed bent on giving away power. To his followers he was in effect consistently saying, *you* heal them, *you* feed them, *you* go forth and preach the good news everywhere and please don't stop someone else who is healing in my name. So, go out two by two and do this in remembrance of me.

As far as St. Paul goes, we find two characteristics of ministry in his early writings. First, ministry is always understood within a community context. Notice, for example, how Paul addresses his letters to the communities at large rather than to any private individual. This seems to imply that all are responsible, although, of course, in different ways and in accord with different gifts. Second, there is real diversity in ministry. Paul, in fact, gives us different lists of such diversity of ministry. In 1 Corinthians, 14:26-28, he shows the centrality of the whole body; in Romans 16:17, he refers to individuals as apostles including Phoebe, but still sees the ministerial gifts as common to all.

This original Pauline vision reflects the primitive house churches of the time. These in turn were modeled on the free, democratic, voluntary associations popular in Paul's day. Research has shown that there was considerable house-centered religion in both the Greco-Roman and Jewish communities. Even the classical authors frequently mention family cult, and archeological excavations have confirmed this. The point worth noting is that Christianity was first nurtured in a nonsacred space, at the heart of daily life in small communities.

This is why it was comfortable then for Paul to mention women as co-workers: Prisca, Phoebe (a deaconess), Mary, Persis, Tryphaena and Tryphosa, Junia and Nympha. Some of these obviously had prominent positions. It is also worth noting that it was the most natural thing in the world that the person who opened his or her house for the gathering of the early church should also be its leader, man or woman. However, a change was shortly in the making. As the church grew, it forsook these limited house-churches and adopted the social order of *households* with its distinctions of order and hierarchy. These were modeled on the Roman patriarchal system. One obvious and immediate result of this move from house churches to household paradigms was the changed status of women to an inferior position, a position later theologized as "God's will." Later, with Constantine, Christianity, now legal and heir to the elaborate pagan temples, adopted the Roman culture of cult. This became reflected in the promotion of

distinctions between clergy and laity and the priesthood—
all of which were further emphasized by a reapplication of
Old Testament themes. In short, the civil Roman empire with
its strict hierarchial and patriarchal paradigms became the
norm for church organization. When bishops eventually got
civil power and certain civic exemptions, the gap between
clergy and laity widened.

Psuedo-Dionysius, writing in the sixth century, had no
trouble using the image of the ladder to describe church
organizational relationship between bishop-presbyter and
laity. Still, for all of this history which we now know in hind-
sight, the vision and ideal of equality, of collaboration, of the
common ministry of the whole church, the people of God,
is enshrined in our Scriptures and tradition and has surfaced
once again in the documents of Vatican II and in the writings
of our own United States bishops.

Attend, for example, to these words from our bishops in
their document *The Catholic Laity: Called and Gifted.* They
write some very "house-church" words, "The adult character
of the people of God flows from baptism and confirmation...
Baptism and confirmation empower all believers to share in
some form of ministry.... This unity of ministry should be
especially evident in the relationships between laity and
clergy as laymen and laywomen respond to the call of the
Spirit in their lives. The clergy help to call forth, identify,
coordinate and affirm the diverse gifts bestowed by the Spirit."
This seems to echo Mary Collins's remark, "In the church's
liturgical tradition, the idea of sacredness and empowerment
arose in the context of baptism, not order."

Of course, as St. Paul reminded us, "the people of God"
phrase with its implications of dialogue, collegiality, and collaboration does not mean that everyone has the same gifts,
talents, and opportunities of office blending into some amor-
phous ecclesiastical glob. The "people of God" concept has
no relationship to that silliness of which only Ph.D.'s are
capable: an equality which flattens everything, as in the instance of a certain free university (now defunct) where

teachers and students sat under the table so no one would be more equal than others. (I would have demanded my money back if that were true.) Equality, rather, is a principle of operation, an approach to mutual respect and recognition.

Such a sensible equality would imply (1) the recognition that each person does in fact have rights which are not conferred but which are innate; (2) that all people have *in principle* access to all roles, responsibilities, and opportunities. Actual circumstances, of course, may rule otherwise: financial circumstances may prevent some blacks from living in certain neighborhoods (and whites too for that matter), but this restriction should never be because they are black; (3) the need for accountability. If people are equal, if all of the baptized, regardless of position or office or virtue, are the people of God, then, contrary to our present system, there must be some accountability on all sides. If we as pastors (or bishops) are not accountable then we have a privilege not sanctioned by the gospel. This is why the revised Code of Canon Law requires the bishop to have a financial council: a symbolic reminder that the diocese is not his private corporation, and that he is accountable.

Finally, we might note that equality implies the recognition of the mutual acknowledgment to the right of self-determination. I know this sounds very political with perhaps overtones of secular feminism, but the fact is that people should not be totally defined by others. The whites of South Africa, for example, should not totally define the limits on blacks, nor should men do the same for women – and vice versa. If you are equal, even though you legitimately differ in office or position, you should have input from others in the light of their feelings, experiences, and history. The presidents and the congresses of our country should not have totally determined the fate of the Indians without dialogue and input. That they did so remains a monument to the paternalistic destruction of an "inferior" and "unequal" people who just happened to be different. That the church of the seven-

teenth century determined a European culture, liturgy, and worship for the "St. Thomas Christians" of India, forcing them to Latinize their old Syro-Chaldaic liturgies, and thereby lost hundreds of thousands to schism, is a monument to a similar paternalistic, one-way monologue and inequality. Recently some Jews resented the anniversary document commemorating *Nostra Aetatae* because they felt they were being defined by the Vatican without their input.

We have much work to do here because while we mentioned Vatical II's implicit and explicit references to the people of God, the documents also affirmed an even greater power of the episcopacy (third chapter on the Constitution of the church) to determine the life of the church. Significantly, as Avery Dulles reminds us, "Vatican II made no allusion to the scholarly magisterium of theologians. Nor did the council make any mention of the consensus of theologians as an authentic source of Christian doctrine. The sense of the faith, of the whole people of God was said to be unerring, but only when the faithful were in agreement with the bishops" *(Lumen Gentium, 12).*[1] It is also noteworthy that even the Synod of Bishops itself is not instituted under the rubric of collegiality, a term used nowhere in this connection, and that the Revised Code treats the synod as advisory to the pope, who has full authority to convoke it and set the agenda. So, even on the level of bishops self-determination is not fully realized, although some made efforts in this direction in the 1985 extraordinary synod called to assess Vatican II.

All this sounds somewhat heady, so again I come back, not so much to the question of principle (which hopefully we would agree with), but of style and approach. If you accept the phrase people of God with all of its implications, then the solo, monarchical, unilateral pastor is not only passé, but un-Christian as well. As we shall see, we do not have to surrender our identity as pastor to be more humane, more consultative. Rather we have to start out precisely building on the gospel principles of dialogue, collegiality, and collaboration in order to be true pastors. We do not have to deny one whit of who and what we are if we approach our style of leadership with the principles of mutual respect. Remember the Foot Washer's words after the fact: "You call me Lord and Master and *that's what I am.*" Having a firm sense of one's position and leadership does not preclude humility: it enhances it.

It would not be amiss in this general context to make the gentle point that in the long run any of us who do have authority and leadership and are sensitive to the ramifications of the people of God are bound to acknowledge the challenge that power puts to us. It is one thing to claim legitimate power, it is another to inspire with power. That is to say, authority without personal witness rings hollow. Our bishops who courageously put out the pastoral on the economy have exercised proper authority, but those who adopt the lifestyles of the poor will inspire beyond that written text. The same with us. What we do will empower what we say. Else we may be open to the judgment: "Their words are bold but their deeds are few. They bind up heavy loads, hard to carry, to lay on other men's shoulders, while they themselves will not lift a finger to budge them" *(Matthew 23.4)*.

Anyway, to return to our point: it would seem that at this time in our history we are being forced into some kind of collaboration, not as a stopgap measure, but as a genuine return to the primitive church model of the people of God. We are agents, we pastors, willing or unwilling, of the hammering out of the old pyramidal structure we have known into the circular structure we discover in the New Testament. This does not do away with wider authority or hierarchy, but it does invite to a new way of perception and leadership.

Notice that in this model of Church as circle we are not doing away with ministries of leadership and authority. As St. Paul wrote, "God has set up in the Church *first* apostles, *second* prophets, *third* teachers" and so on *(1 Corinthians 12:28)*. Rather, a circle makes Jesus' call to every Christian more visible, and thus more available for service to the Church. At the same time the circle

enables everyone in the Church to communicate more
effectively with those whose special calling is to lead.
Finally, the circle model reminds those who lead that
they are servants, "servants of the servants of God" as
Pope Gregory the Great 14 centuries ago defined the role
of the popes. [2]

So, in summary, we are invited to a style of leadership that
moves:

1. from power to service
2. from dictatorial to participatory
3. from closed to accountable
4. from presumed to earned
5. from privilege to access
6. from solo to collaborative.

As Archbishop Robert Sanchez said in 1984 at the
centenary celebration of the Third Plenary Council of Baltimore:

> It may perhaps sound simplistic, but I do believe that
> Our Holy Father, the Vicar of Christ on his earth, models
> for the Church world the style of leadership. One hun-
> dred years ago that model was monarchical. Pope Pius
> IX, strengthened by the declaration of infallability, had
> declared himself a prisoner of the Vatican. He was in-
> deed inaccessible. This leadership style had its own
> reflection in the hierarchy of our country, as well as the
> ministry of our priests and religious. The distinction
> between the clergy and laity was most clear. Given this
> style of leadership, it is easy to understand the reserva-
> tions and doubts which the clergy and hierarchy of that
> age entertained regarding the efforts of the laity to share
> ministry. The experience with trusteeism had left
> unpleasant feelings in the hearts of the hierarchy and
> clergy of the time.

> Today, this style of leadership has changed. During the
> Second Vatican Council, Pope John XXIII said: "You
> have come to call this Council...you are talking and
> I am listening." The role model of leadership had
> changed; now the Pope listens; collegiality was restored.
> This is the presidential model; the leader presides and

he listens. Thus, the Council of Fathers of Vatican II offered to us a collegial form of Church government. Whereas 100 years ago, the principal sacrament was Holy Order, today we see that Baptism is central to our theology. Now we speak of the priesthood of all the faithful."[3]

Again, all this does not necessarily in any way devalue leadership but rather positions it within a basic gospel context.

There are all kinds of theories of leadership and many books on group, corporate, and church management. But no matter what the theory, as the authors of the popular book, *In Search of Excellence*, emphasized, leadership is crucial. I tend to adopt the theory of Rabbi Edwin Friedman, a family therapist, who sees the same dynamics working in churches and synagogues, as well as in families; namely, that "if the leader can define himself or herself really well, express his or her goals, differentiate himself out of the anxiety of the system, and so on, it will affect the entire organization. . . . The head of a family of three people and the head of a huge organization have as much effect on the rest of the body."[4] He argues that we, in all respects—politically and ecclesiastically—place too much emphasis on information and knowledge and too little on the functioning of the leader (bishops, please note). And, to this extent, he is opposed to leadership by consensus.

I agree. Too often shared and collaborative ministry translates as finding the lowest common denominator. There's a world of difference between listening and consensus, the latter strongly implying majority vote. Can you image Jesus leading that way? Can you image him saying, "All right, you guys, gather 'round. We're going to make a breakthrough today. What're your thoughts on the Samaritans? What's that, Peter? No, killing the bastards isn't what I had in mind. Well, maybe we're not ready for that one. How about a consensus on tax collectors, those outside the law, women?" You see, we think that there are only two alternatives: consensus and authoritarianism. There's a third way. Listen to Friedman:

There's a third alternative to functioning either in a
charismatic or authoritarian way or in a consensus style.
The third alternative is: "Be yourself. Keep defining yourself and saying what you believe." And not because
you're trying to get everybody to move, but just because
you're the leader, they are more likely to go along with
you than if you get into a will struggle with them. And
it's less enervating. People often claim it's possible to get
rid of the problems of authoritarianism and too much
reliance on the leader by having a consensus. But the
world's greatest ideas did not come from consensus
groups, they came from people in their own solitude.
Whitehead defined religion as what one does with one's
own solitude. The prophet doesn't hear the call in the
crowd. The muse doesn't strike people in the subway. [5]

We must be careful not to distort Friedman's meaning. He
is not saying that the lone dictator is the style. He is saying
very emphatically that the leader must keep in touch and
that's the key. It's a kind of rhythm of fusing and leaving, of
listening often, intently, and respectfully but then retreating
into solitude. ("One of those days Jesus went out into the hills
to pray and spent the whole night praying to God." *(Luke 6:12).*
"Jesus knowing that they intended to come and make him
king by force, withdrew again into the hills by himself" *(John
6:15).* In more religious terms which would be compatible
with us, our leadership must be a constant movement between ministry and contemplation. Authoritarianism may kill
the people, but consensus kills the prophet.

As we close with all of our talk about the people of God
and its components of dialogue, collaboration, and collegiality
as defining our style of leadership, we can see that we are
really being led to examine the whole question of priestly
spirituality. Here's a rock bottom issue, and it is here, I suggest, that we will discover the delicate resolution of the tension between authority and service.

Furthermore, although the reader will perceive a sympathy for feminine concerns and voices of spirituality in this
book, I think that we also need to hear Father Patrick Ar-

nold's warning against "unbalanced feminine valuing" threatening to domesticate God, making him a benign, harmless, sympathetic household god. He is saying – and rejoices in the fact – that feminine emphasis on God's qualities of community, compassion, kindness, and gentleness is a welcomed counterpoint to the overly legalistic, authoritarian, and partiarchal concept of God and the church structures that promote such an image. He is simply concerned about any exclusive overemphasis that reduces God to a benign grandfather and that supresses the equally valid "masculine" voice of spirtuality.

What is that masculine voice? It is the voice that commanded Abraham to leave his native land; the voice of Hosea who confronted his people's degenerate faith; the voice of Second Isaiah who offered Israel a strong new vision; the voice of Paul breaking ethnic barriers of the old religion; the voices of Dorothy Day, Daniel Berrigan, and Theresa Kane; the voice, finally, of Jesus who called for the sword, not peace, and demanded that we leave all for the sake of the kingdom.

In our context of talking about leadership, then, our masculine voices should absolutely be modified by the feminine voices speaking today and yesterday, but they should not be intimidated or suppressed, for the masculine voices, in spirituality and leadership, may also be the sounds of God speaking.

A wealthy woman from Philadelphia gave a grand party one evening. Among her guests was the Cardinal Archibishop. At one point during the dinner, the hostess was horrified to note that the butler—a family servant of many years' standing and of impeccable manners—was behaving quite oddly, swaying on his feet, stumbling about, and nearly dropping serving dishes. Furious, she quickly scribbled a note to him and placed it on the butler's tray. It read: "You are drunk. Leave

the room immediately." Whereupon the
butler, with a suavity and dignity born of
years of service, moved down the table and
gracefully laid the note on the plate of the
Cardinal Archbishop.

*As the banquet was about to begin, the chairman
realized that the priest had not yet arrived to give
the invocation. He whispered to the main speaker,
"Sir, since the priest hasn't come, will you please
ask the blessing?" The speaker arose, bowed his
head, and with deep feeling said, "There being no
priest present, let us thank God."*

VII

Context
for Collaboration

"I WANT YOU CHILDREN, "MONSIGNOR SAID, " TO LOOK AT THIS MAN'S
hands." "This man" happened to be the janitor Monsignor
brought with him when he dropped by for a classroom visit.
The janitor, obviously embarrassed, but an obedient member
of the flock held out his palms for us to see.

They were the type of hands, I thought, that marked you
for immediate dismissal from the dinner table. They were
calloused and dirty.

Monsignor held the man's right hand up for us to see.
"These hands," he said, "do the Lord's work." Some of us no
doubt thought of those very same hands grasping a mop to
clean up a third-grader's spilled lunch and wondered about
the extent of the Lord's interest in the task.

"'This man's hands," Monsignor continued, "have cleaned our church, kept your school running and have washed the statues of Jesus, Mary and Joseph that grace our lawn. This man's hands – this man's life – are dedicated to the Lord in each and everything he does. Take a good look at your hands and see that they do the same.'"[1]

Thus a homely and pointed reminder to the children of an earlier age of the vocation of the laity. And if we are to talk at all in the next chapter about the principles of collaboration with the laity, we must begin with a firm sense of where their vocation primarily lies and of the innate dignity of that vocation. For the fact is that even after all these years we and the people themselves see very little value in their daily work; especially, as Studs Terkel says in his book, *Working,* if people are haunted by planned obsolescence and the fear of no longer being needed in a world of needless things. On the contrary, to become a priest or a lay minister dedicated to full-time service to the Lord is still seen as a far better and guaranteed road to spirituality than to be a mechanic or a carpenter.

From the pinnacle of full-time church work, everything else seems to devolve in descending order of unworthiness as far as holiness goes. If you made time and were devout you could squeeze in some spirituality on Sunday, but never in the real world. Even our retreats for lay people gave this message by focusing mainly on prayer and the sacraments and seldom on the gifts the people had given for public service and witness. As the authors of *Finding a Job You Can Love* [2] write, "Unfortunately, it is still common for Christians to feel that increased church activity equals heightened spirituality" (p. 16). This unconscious spiritual caste system must be recognized as we multiply degreed lay ministers and what we call "sanctuary" ministers and volunteers (those primarily or exclusively devoted to parish work and organizations). Furthermore, "Failing to distinguish between life as an institution and life in the world through its members, churches are too often

concerned with their institutional roles. When that happens,
they end up working primarily for their own survival and
growth" (p. 19). How true that is. How often we fall into self-
analysis and self-survival techniques with no concept of what
it means to be church where the vast arena of life and witness
is for the average person. As the 1977 Declaration of Christian Concern issued by the Chicago Catholics stated:

> While many in the church exhaust their energies argu-
> ing internal issues, albeit important ones, such as ordina-
> tion of women and married clergy, the laity who spend
> most of their time and energy in the professional
> and occupational world, appear to have been
> deserted. . . . Who now sustains lay persons as they meet
> the daily challenges of their jobs and professions? . . .

Father Jerry Foley from Minnesota expresses the same
thought this way:

> At Vatican Council II, the bishops reclaimed this vision
> of the early church when they gave us the first conciliar
> document ever written on the role of the laity. They
> declared that the people are the church and that all peo-
> ple are called to ministry through baptism. These
> ministries, they stated, are not restricted to various forms
> of service within the faith community; rather, the laity's
> unique role is to make the church present in the world,
> to transform political, economic, and social institutions
> in the light of the gospel.

> Despite this vision, our institutional model of church has
> continued strongly to influence our sense of ministry,
> leading us to perceive lay ministry as a sharing in the
> ministry of clerics.[3]

The fact is that we have not yet developed any kind of
theology of work, and until we do, much that currently goes
under the name of ministry is really in-house inflation. We
have to try to come up with answers to Joe Holland's questions, "mechanics, taxi drivers, lawyers, clerk-typists, computer programmers, flight attendants, teachers, doctors, trash

collectors, parents, waitresses, orderlies. . . . What do these have in common? They are all names for ways in which we humans work. What, then, is the theological meaning of work?"[4]

Because at the moment we really have no adequate answer to this question, working people have little or no sense that their work is either "vocational" or in any way related to the kingdom of God. Listen to Father Thomas McMahon, professor of business ethics at Loyola University in Chicago. He was interviewed by the editors of *Salt,* a social justice publication. The discussion centered around ethics. Here's an excerpt:

> Can a good Christian business executive really mix faith with work?
>
> I hope so, but there's no straight answer on this. I'm doing a survey in which I'm finding out that often people's religious convictions don't mix well with their business dealings.
>
> Why?
>
> For one thing, some people don't think what they're doing is holy. When people work, it's more than just production or management or something like that. What they're doing is vocation—they've got a calling.
>
> When they change raw materials into something that's useful to people, that's co-creation.
>
> When they conserve raw materials instead of wasting them, that's co-conservation. Workers have to have more self-esteem and realize that what they're doing is in fact holy.
>
> How can people begin to see their work as holy?
>
> Well, one way is by publicizing: by writing articles about it, preaching about it, teaching it in CCD and other places.
>
> Work really needs to be talked about in the churches and schools. The only time these executives hear from priests is when they want to fix the books, or for a pro-

gram of some kind. When was the last time you heard
a sermon on the vocation of business executives?

Once I spoke with one of the vice presidents of a large
publishing firm in Chicago, and he was Catholic. At first
this guy was being polite, you know, by giving me all
the signs that he wasn't really interested in helping me
with the survey. But once he began to open up, it made
all the difference in the world. This guy said, "Father,
I've been working here 25 years, and this is the first time
a priest ever asked me what I do, what did I think about
the role of my religion in work. You're the first priest
to come and see me."

Before people can bring this witness or whatever you
want to call it, people need to see themselves in this light:
that what they're doing has value.

When we can come to terms with work as a value, as an active participation in God's creative presence, then we can gain
a better perspective of shared and collaborative ministry as
something inclusive of, but of pointing beyond, the parish
or church institution — and that's the fundamental message of
this chapter. As Pope John Paul II has reminded us: "Before
the Second Vatican Council the concept of 'vocation' was
applied first of all to the priesthood and religious life. . . .
The council has broadened this way of looking at
things. . . [through] the renewed awareness of the universal
sharing of all the baptised in Christ's threefold prophetic,
priestly and kingly mission." "And he said in his encyclical
On Human Work that the laity have a "duty to form a spirituality of work which will help all people come closer, through
work, to God." Bishop James Hoffman of Toledo, chairman
of the Bishop's Committee on the Laity, put it forcefully:

I am not opposed to lay people becoming more involved
in the ministries of the church. But that is not their
primary role. For example, some of our people are executives in multinational corporations and cannot serve
on the parish council because they may be in Munich
on Tuesday when it meets. But if they have an impact
on what these corporations are doing, that is their role.

Writer Kenneth Guentert says it all more colloquially:

> I'm not against priests. I like them, as men and as an
> idea. The more cultic the better. I like the Eucharist and
> the sacraments. That's why I'm Catholic. It's just that the
> priestly function, as basic as it is to the Catholic religion,
> takes only the better part of an hour each week. When
> the priest says, Go, the Mass is ended, the Mass ends.
> Period. Finito. The rest of the week—all 167 hours of it—
> belongs to the laity. . . . What we have here is a voca-
> tion crisis—a shortage of qualified laypeople. A qualified
> layperson is any nonprofessional Catholic with the im-
> agination to connect the creative work of his or her life
> to the creative work of God.

There are, then, several approaches we can keep in mind
before we discuss our principles of collaboration. The first
is to ponder these words:

> By changing the day of worship to Sunday, the beginning
> of the week, the early church made a powerful state-
> ment that the faith community comes together not as
> an end of itself, but to prepare members for their week
> in the world. Sunday was seen not as a day of rest or
> escape, but as a day of preparation for mission. We must
> find ways to help Catholics today leave Mass feeling that
> their daily lives at work and in the home are important
> to their faith.[5]

Secondly, we must pay attention to our attitude and that of
our staff and our sanctuary ministers—and that attitude (and
indoctrination, if you want) must be one of service. I know
that sounds prosaic, but it's important to grasp. I mean, for
example, that the eucharistic minister who brings communion to the hospital patient is not only reaching out from the
larger community to the sick in a most powerful gesture, but
that in a very significant way, the patient himself or herself
is being healed and prayed for so as to be returned to the
world in renewed witness, wisdom, and power. You see, the
emphasis here is not so much on the eucharistic minister, as
on the patient who is being given the message that he or she

is the important one and that his or her contribution to the world is valuable.

Or, to put it another way, the message is not that the sickness may not indeed be a blessing in disguise, so that this person can get some deserved rest and an opportunity to rethink life's priorities, but that the sickness is a potential time of empowerment for daily holiness in the world. In a word, the minister must not see himself or herself as superior for bringing the eucharist from the sanctuary, but rather as a servant-catalyst in restoring the vocation of another to a rightful place in the world. It's a critical attitude that carefully relfects the words of *Evangelii Nuntiandi (70)*: "'The primary and immediate task [of the laity] is not to establish and develop the ecclesial community—this is the specific role of the pastors—but to put to use every Christian and evangelical possibility latent but already present and active in the affairs of the world."

Accordingly, years ago when I used to give the Cana Conferences to married couples, I would always remind parents that according to Jesus they have, above all the others, the best chance of salvation. Why? Because in the famous Matthew 25 passage, Jesus gives us the only measurements for salvation—and all of them "in the world!" They are what we call today the corporal and spiritual works of mercy. The beautiful part, I reminded the parents, is that they're built right into secular, worldly, family life. You can't escape them if you wanted to. Parents, in raising children, can't avoid heaven. Feeding the hungry, giving drink to the thirsty, etc. They're all right there in the home (not the sanctuary). So, for example, in schematic form, it works like this:

2 a.m. bottle—giving drink to the thirsty.
diapering—clothing the naked.
cough medicine to the bedroom—visiting the sick.
preparing meals—feeding the hungry.
Dad, can you help me with my homework—instructing the
    ignorant.

Mom, what'll I wear?—counseling the doubtful.
the cat died—burying the dead.
hearing the kid's prayer—praying for the living and the dead
     (endlessly).
are you still in the bathroom?—visiting the imprisoned.

This is not a digression. The reality is that most Catholics, like most other human beings, live in the world for the greater part of their lives. They don't have all the time to do churchy things. We cannot and should not measure their standing or their commitment by whether they're teaching CCD or ushering at Sunday Mass. They ought not to be thought of as second class Catholics. They need our affirmation. Dorothy Sayers once remarked that it is unfortunate that a carpenter hears this on Sunday. "Don't get drunk on Saturday and be sure to give enough in the collection"—instead of hearing, "Be the best carpenter you can be." In this vein, Archbishop McCarthy of Miami is right when he comments, "The laity need to be aroused to a great sense of responsibility, to recover their early Christian, more prominent role in transforming society in the name of the church. They should not have to depend on the urging of the clerical celibates to be committed to renewing family life. They should not have to wait for the bishops to inaugurate questions about ethics in the economy."[6] There's also an insightful letter to the editor from a lay woman who, along these lines, probes deeper and so offers us a challenge:

> "Young Professionals Juggle Religion and Their Careers" [Oct. 23] pointed out conflicts between work and religious observance and cited creative ways of solving them. However, the examples dealt only with religious externals and did not involve essential conflicts between faith and work.
>
> A Buddhist or Quaker (and others) might ask,"Does the good job with the advertising agency promoting unnecessary consumption constitute "right work," or how can I work for a company that in some part services the war machine? These are questions of conscience that go

deeper and are more difficult to reconcile than observ-
ing dietery laws or adjusting religious holiday
timetables.[7]

At the risk of some overkill, since we are really burdened
with the centuries-old dualism between the sacred and the
secular, let me quote as a kind of summary of our thoughts
so far, the lengthy but wise observations of Frank Staropoli
entitled, "What Does It Mean to be a 'Layperson'?":

It's been fascinating to watch over the years the different
responses of people to my work "in the Church." When
I moved from the management of a small family
business eight years ago to paid Church ministry with
my wife Sue (co-directing the diocesan Family Life Office), people treated me differently. This was most
peculiar and puzzling to me at first, but I've since come
to understand that the root of the reaction is a distorted
understanding of what it means to be a lay person. I'd
call this an "inverted vision" and I believe it exists in most
people, lay, clergy or religious.

We lay folk tend to believe that involvement in the
parish council, committees, liturgical ministries, etc., are
the hallmarks of a truly committed Christian. We seek
and cherish these "extra-ordinary" roles as though they
were our primary responses to the Lord. We fail to
understand that our commitment through baptism is to
be *in the world,* involved in our ordinary roles at home,
at work and in our communities. The problem is that
those other parish ministries, while also valid ministries,
are seen as our primary response to the Lord. In this
sense, then, we have inverted vision.

Parish, diocesan and national leaders often hold a
similarly distorted understanding of what it means to be
a lay person. These leadership people (lay, clergy or
religious) focus time, talent and treasure on the task of
getting people involved in the parish. Not only are lay
people lacking explicit support in our ordinary worldy
mission, but our leaders' efforts to involve us in the extraordinary may often become a distraction. In this
sense, then, the inverted vision of the laity is reinforced
by our church leaders.

How might the institutional church define its role in relation to the laity? A line of logic might go like this: (1) The mission of the church, the people of God, is to be in the world—a leaven society. (2) The laity as church are the ordinary contact point with the world and the primary concrete instruments of that mission as we live—at home, in neighborhoods, on jobs and in community organizations. (3) The role of the institutional Church is to support the laity in this mission in the world.

Therefore, the bishops, a parish council or committee members, a pastor or any other leader can measure the worth of her/his endeavors by this standard: *To what degree does my ministry empower the laity to live their faith in the world?*

This will mean a new series of questions to be asked of the laity, a listening process which does not focus on "Do you prefer having mass at 9:00 or 9:30?" and "Which parish committee would you be interested in joining?" The questions instead need to be non-directive and non-churchy, e.g. "What's happening in your life? What's on your mind? What's your agenda?"

Current adult education and lay ministry training programs need to be carefully evaluated. I'd ask, for example, would the training have helped me to understand earlier in my marriage how to communicate with my wife?. . .Would it have helped me recognize my Christian mission as a business executive?. . .Will your training help me now as my family and I discern our direction for the future?

We, the laity, have our own shifting to do. We have to break out of our still-operative identification of the "Church" as the buildings, the pastor, the council, the programs, etc. . . .The role of the institutional church will be to assist us in discovering the depth of faith, prayer and response to the Lord already alive in us—at home, at work, and in the world.[8]

All of the foregoing must cause us to reflect once more on the theory and the theology from which we're operating as pastors or parishes. If our model of parish is a closed one with grace, information, direction, and power trickling down from

the top, then we will never empower people for their place
in the world. We will merely (and with some satisfaction) pull
them into our churchy structures as voluntary and obedient
extensions of ourselves – with all of the implied reward and
status. By equating a "good" Catholic with proximity to the
sanctuary, we not only fail to challenge the laity in their roles
in the world, but we actually keep them infantile; we make
them feel that on the really bedrock religious level we will
take care to them, for it is with us and our churchy formulas
and rituals to which they are privy that spiritual power and
salvation ultimately rests.

But if our model of parish is open, then our primary movement is not from the top down but from "in and out." "People
move *through* the church into the world; in or out is not as
important as in and out. . . . A central characteristic of the
open church is that both clergy and laity are seen as
ministers. . . . The clergy are the leaders and organizers of the
church – a training-and-equipping instituion."[9]

This, then, is the burden of our chapter on the context
for collaboration. It's a matter of perspective as we have so
often said, a matter of sitting back and asking ourselves as
pastors, "What are we about? What part does the parish play
in the larger lives of the people? How can I and all parish
ministers aid the people struggling with their daily lives? What
affirmations, encouragements, and celebrations will help
them to realize most fully their status in the world as the people of God?"

Old thorns and old priests should be left alone:
there's power in the pair of them if they want to
use it. You may not believe it, but there was a
time in Ireland when everyone believed it and
maybe they were right. It's better to be sure than
sorry.

*Anyhow, there was this fellow one time and he
was very fond of the drink. Worse still he had a
wife and a family, and the way he was drinking
himself out of house and habitation they were living on the clippings of tin, licking the stones. She
was sick, sore, and tired scolding him and asking
him to have sense, so in the later end she went
to the old parish priest about him.*

*The parish priest listened to her story and
said he would see what he could do. So this day
there was a market or something in the village
and the priest knew her man would be there and
wouldn't leave the public house till he lowered
every cent in his pocket down the red lane, and
maybe rise more on the slate if his name was
good.*

*So the priest was in the village and he seen
her man heading for the public house. He called
him over.*

"I forbid you to go in there this day," says he.

*"Only one drink, Father," says he, "and then
I'm going home to my wife and children."*

*"One drink," says the priest, "will lead to
another drink and another and another till you go
home with the two legs plaiting under you. Now
listen here," says the priest, "I don't want to use
my power, but if you go inside that public house
today or let drink wet your lips, I'll turn you into
a mouse by twelve o'clock tonight."*

*At that the priest turned and walked away
home, and her man turned and walked home too.
He didn't want to draw the anger of the priest on
him and believed he had the power when he
wanted.*

*He wasn't far outside the village on his way
home and who does he meet but an old pal who'd
been years in England or America and was just
home. Well, you know how it is. Handshakes and
great talk and what not. And before her man
knew where he was, he was back with this pal in*

the pub in the village and didn't leave it till he
couldn't see a hole in a ladder.

It was dark, down night when he got as far
as his own house and his wife, Mary, was sitting
lamenting to herself at the fire. He staggered in
and looked at the mantelpiece and he could see
the clock all right but he was that cross-eyed with
drink he couldn't tell what time it was.

"Mary," says he, "what time is it?"

"What time do you think?" says she. "It's a
few minutes off midnight."

"Mary," says he, "if you see me getting wee
and hairy...put out that bloody cat."[10]

A Protestant version we can resonate with: Mr. Wilson seldom went to church, always finding some excuse, but one Sunday he was asked to greet the arrivals at the door and his wife succeeded in inducing him to go and meet his obligation. Extending his hand to a well-dressed young man, he said, "Nice to see you here. Glad you could make it." "I usually manage to get here," replied the young man as he walked up to the pulpit and began the service.

VIII

Principles
of Collaboration

PAYING TRIBUTE TO OUR CATHOLIC FONDNESS FOR MYSTICAL NUMBERS, let me share in this chapter what I think are seven essential attitudes or unwritten perimeters that form the inviting atmosphere for shared and collaborative ministry.

The first attitude is to create an appreciation for our native tradition. In spite of what we may remember about the abuse of lay trusteeism in the United States, the fact is that the laity, from the beginning and by necessity, were quite active in local church affairs. After all, the people, contrary to their European experience, had no governmental support for their religion in this country. The laity, therefore, had to build and

108

sustain their own religious institutions, especially since they often preceded the clergy to these shores. And with the pay, of course, went the say; and from this experience, early on, there arose a long democratic tradition of lay sharing. It wasn't until 1829 that there emerged any kind of strong, centralized episcopal power. (It also might be out of place here to remember that this country had not had a resident bishop for 150 years, and that the first two were democratically elected by their peers.) It is, therefore, a return to our native tradition for lay people once more to reclaim active participation in parish life. Accordingly, the 1984 Notre Dame Report on Parish Life is simply underscoring that tradition when it says:

> If a major purpose of Vatican II was to reinstate the sense that all Christians—lay, priests and religious—are responsible for the corporate life of the church in the local parish, Vatican II is succeeding in the United States. The American church is participatory not only in religious ritual but especially in shared responsibility for ministry. Even in ritual, people have noticed how much more active and expressive they are expected to be. Parish policy-making and governance patterns are not yet clearly demonstrated but the effort to find parish governance mechanisms as effective or more effective than parish councils continues.[1]

So we are not really breaking such new ground as we think. We are rather reclaiming some old ground, and it might be well to instruct our people in their own national ecclesiastical history to broaden their attitudes and understanding of who they have been so they can accept the challenge of becoming who they should be.[2]

The second attitude is vision. I mean, of course, our vision of church as translated on the parish level. We have referred to this in the last chapter, and once again we must ask ourselves, what are we in business for? How do we organize our common life, how do we see ourselves? The answers to these questions will be reflected in our lifestyle, our community priorities, the very architecture of the "plant." If you want an unfailing clue as to the accepted perception of your parish, just try out a little word association. When someone says the name of your parish aloud, what images cluster? Great bingos? Paid off mortgage? Last year's basketball champs? These are all pretty good (and desirable) but if that is *all* that comes to mind, if that is *all* that clusters, then you might as well be running the YM/YWCA. If, however, our vision of parish is one in which the whole community is basically ministerial, a living sign of the compassionate and celebrating Christ, then at least we can move out from there to find proper expressions. Also, in this context, numbers just don't assume the importance that they seem to have for so many priests (and bishops) who have been co-opted by the American Dream Standard where bigger is always better.

We are usually unnerved, as are our Protestant brothers and sisters, when we mutually discuss numbers. They talk of church membership in terms of individuals and we in terms of entire families. We can't understand how they can do anything with a mere, say, 250 individuals (notice our criterion of *doing*), and they can't understand how we can minister to 2500 families. One Protestant minister has come up with this formula for the relationship between numbers and their pastoral characteristics:

> Very small congregations of 75 members—a tight knit group
>
> Small (75 - 200)—familiar faces; dominant core group
>
> Middle sized (200-300)—full-time pastor; full program
>
> Moderately large (350 - 800)—diverse fellowship and program
>
> Very large (800 or over)—comprehensive program; specialized staff[3]

Remember, these are all numbers in terms of individuals. I don't know what he would think of parishes of 5,000 or more people. The point here is, we should worry less about boosting

the census and more about who and what we are regardless
of numbers—recalling to mind the first design of one Master
and the twelve disciples. It's a matter of giving priority to internal vision, not external numbers. And this emphasis in turn
forces us back once more to the whole area of spirituality
for, as Henri Nowen has put it, "To contemplate is to see and
to minister is to make visible" what we see. I guess I'm saying that the attitude of vision is really the issue of spirituality,
gospel mandate, and contemplation, and all will flow from
that, including the kind of shared and collaborative ministry
we bring forth.

The third attitude is related to vision; it is listening. As we
said in the section on leadership, the good leader is not only
grounded in his or her own vision but also in the testing of
that vision by listening. There are many forms and many
forums for listening, from dialogue to parish newsletters to
parish town-hall type meetings. In our parish, we have a half
dozen or so standard ways of listening besides our presence
at all weekend liturgies and one-on-one conversations. We
have, for example, a suggestion box in our church vestibule.
We put out a quarterly newspaper and ask the parish council members to listen carefully and bring things back to our
attention. On the third Sunday of the month at the noontime
Mass, we have a dialogue homily—a real give and take on
issues that concern everybody. We make neighborhood visita-
tions once a month.

In addition to these, there are two other ways which may
be somewhat unusual. On every Saturday evening of the year
(except the summertime), I invite couples in for dinner
(couples being married, single, widowed). In a long
bachelorhood, I have learned to cook tolerably well and, by
choice, I do not have a housekeeper—just a cleaning woman
who comes in once a week to ward off the board of health.
I have found this a wonderful way to meet people, especially
spouses of other traditions. You cannot eat and drink with
people and not listen and learn. It's not only fun having peo-

ple in for dinner, but it's a form of basic hospitality, a quite practical, theological way of truly discovering Christ "in the breaking of the bread."

The other way we have listened and learned and discerned is by means of the type of census we put out a few years ago.[4] Besides the usual statistical information on a sheet, which was torn off and mailed in, we had about ten other anonymous pages whereby at least three members of a household could respond. Here are some typical examples on our census:

I find most meaning in attending Mass at:

Person A	Person B	Person C
____St. Mary's	____St. Mary's	____St. Mary's
____another local church	____another local church	____another local church
____a local chapel, campus	____a local chapel, campus	____a local chapel campus
____a church in another town	____a church in another town	____a church in another town

Three people had a chance to give an opinion. Thus, more examples:

At Mass I most prefer: ____no music ____only organ music ____the choir singing ____folk music ____congregational singing.

The last time I talked with my parish priest in person or over the phone was ____in the past two days ____in the past week ____in the past month ____in the past six months ____in the past five years or more ____never.

My feeling about St. Mary's: homilies, music, lectors, CCD program, banners, flowers, decorations, parish organizations, etc. is:

____very good ____good ____fair ____poor ____indifferent

Then we had fill-ins, like when you were at school. Here are some examples:

"Something I've always wanted to say to the pastor is ___."
"What do you think of the pastor (associate pastor)?" ___."
"I think the parish should _____."
"I think the biggest problem we have to face today is ___."
"Something we never hear preached, but should, is ___."

We learned a lot from this way of listening.[5]

The fourth attitude inviting shared and collaborative ministry is the appreciation of the power of education. So many people, even twenty-five years later, don't have any notion of the reasons behind the changes wrought by Vatican II. True enough, as Americans we are a peculiarly ahistorical people. Still, we do have a literate and educated congregation who would benefit from some intellectual and historical underpinnings of what is happening in the church. They need a fuller grasp of the Catholic tradition to help them make sense out of the present confusion. In response to this need, we have found a high readership of Sunday bulletin inserts, our own or the professional ones. Courses and instructional homilies can educate and give the people a sense of place, time, and tradition in the church.

The fifth attitude means that we should never consciously create a two-tiered congregation of "ins" and "outs." We can do this by insisting on uniformity, by being intolerant of other forms of traditional worship and expression that might not be to our updated liking.

The sixth attitude is that good liturgy softens. One of the things we learn from the business world is that often, if you can't persuade others intellectually to like your idea, you can at least make them less hostile if the execution of that idea is tastefully and sensitively done. So, the strategy is that, for those who dislike the "new" liturgy and hanker after the old, you can at least make the former as lovely and religious an experience as possible. The hope is that those who fondly remember the past will perhaps at least admit that, while the present is not their cup of tea, it is in fact kind of nice. *The seventh and last attitude* is a conviction of the merits of cross-pollination. By this I mean that parish leadership should presume that most parishioners know their immediate group or neighborhood but not others of the congregation. One of the main goals of the pastor and staff, it seems to me, is to provide ways and means for people from "across town" to meet one another and get involved in mutual tasks.

These, then, are seven "atmospheric" attitudes, like a perfume in the air, that ought to be the infrastructure of shared and collaborative ministry. But, now, after that, what? How do you get people involved? Allow me to suggest five principles that I have found helpful.

1. The "one-shot piggyback." By this principle I mean that the pastor—he is still a very key figure, remember—will ask someone to host an event; say, for example, the Advent Communal Confession. After that person or couple faints and is revived in spasms of protested inadequacy, the pastor can usually calm them down and win them over by reminding them that it's only for one time and they can revert to the cloister afterwards. Just knowing that it's one time only and will be quickly over with is a strong point of consideration. But then they are told of the "piggyback." That is, last year's host or couple will help them, has a log of what to do, and their only obligation is to help next year's host. The presence of experienced people is reassuring and most often the clinching point of acceptance. (Of course, this means that in starting out, you or a parish minister will have to spend a great deal of time helping, teaching, and inspiring the initial couples.)

2. The "Glenmary Dance" is the second principle. You know that the Glenmary missionaries go into an area, start a parish and, as soon as it is self-sufficient with a native pastor, they pull out. Applied to soliciting ministers, it means that you do a lot of teaching and demonstrating in the first years and then gradually turn the event over to others while you slowly but firmly "dance away," leaving the ministry in their hands. For example, I wanted to show the people that there was more than one official way to pray publicly, namely, the sacraments and the Divine Office, in addition to the Mass. (In a practical way, I was also readying them for the possibility of fewer priests someday.) So I asked those who came to daily Mass if they would experiment with learning the Office. I gave them background and history and then eventually practice. Little by little we were able to replace Mass once a week with an alternate form with me leading the service. Gradually, lay people were encouraged to lead (not that radical, the office started with a group of laymen, the monks). I then began to sit in the front pew, then the middle, then the last pew, and, finally, I went out the front door. My "Glenmary Dance" enabled the people to claim a ministry of public prayer. It's an example of what the Whiteheads describe as nurturing the group's effectiveness.

3. *"Happy Endings"* is the third principle. People (especially volunteers) should not have to think that they're in some position eternally. At times people really want out but don't want to let Father down. Or it may be simply a time for them to grow in other areas. Besides, you don't want a clique to form. So anyone in office, anyone who is the head of a parish organization is in for two years, and, in the course of the second year, they must train their successor. There must be some legitimizing way to bow out or move leadership along.

4. *The fourth principle is R.S.V.P.* This means that you, the pastor, *invite* people individually and personally, as opposed to seeking volunteers. The mystique of the pastor is still strong, and people don't like to refuse. Besides, in asking for volunteers, you know who you're going to get: the same old faithful ones who unwittingly claim all the territory and intimidate others who don't want to infringe. A further note about volunteers is that there is no gracious way to un-invite the incompetent ones. Personal invitation is better.

5. *Finally, there is "No Strings Education."* There are always, within decent travel time for most people, all kinds of educa-

tional opportunities. For many years we've had the policy that for anyone who wants to go to a workshop or seminar or whatever (within reason), the parish will pick up all or most of the tab. Lucien Deiss or Raymond Brown or the like may be in the area or within traveling distance. We will pay people's way to go. But here's the point: there are no strings attached. They do not have to report back. They do not have to get involved. They do not have to do anything. The idea is that if they catch fire, get some new insight, eventually they will enrich the parish as a whole. We haven't had that many takers over the past dozen years—maybe about twelve to fifteen. Still, that's about 120 to 150 people who have been exposed to some powerful and wonderful ideas and people, and that's got to impact the parish somehow and in some way.

So these are the seven attitudes and five principles of practical shared ministry. They are not world-shaking but rather more like common sense applications. And they are not unique. In some form or other big business uses them. They are simply human ways to nurture commitment and foster collaboration.

One of Madeleine L'Engle's lovely short stories is entitled "The Sphinx at Dawn." It's the classical encounter, from Greek mythology, between the desert Sphinx and, this time, the "young king," the Christ Child. As usual, the Sphinx asks riddles, as he did to Oedipus on his way from Corinth to Thebes. To fail to answer the riddle is to forfeit one's life. The Child, the "young king", with the help of his worldly-wise camel, answers all of them. At last the Child asks, "Is there another riddle?" The Sphinx answers, "Yes, there is the final riddle. What do you have that I will keep forever and ever and beyond the time my stone has crumbled into sand and beyond that again?" In response, the boy runs to the Sphinx, climbs up her side until he reaches the great head, and says, "This is what you will keep"—and he gave her a kiss. "You will keep my love." The Sphinx says simply, "'That is always your answer, isn't it? The most difficult answer of all.'"[6]

This moving scene challenges us here—at least to this extent: all that we have seen so far is well and good, but now, the most difficult answer of all is awaiting the questions: "How do you work it out in practice? How does the vision translate?" I can only share briefly as we close this chapter *some* ways that I know. Others have been more creative, and you and I will have to learn from them. For the moment, then, I will pull in some suggestions from my previous books, along with some new ones, to give broad, twofold areas of practical collaboration, what I call "The collaboration of place and the collaboration of subsidiarity."

The collaboration of place simply means that as community leaders and administrators of the "plant" we can do many little things that make the church property as communal as possible and by so doing promote a sense of sharing and co-ownership. Such not-so-world-shaking things might be:

1. *In an open-door policy,* leave as many doors unlocked all the time as possible. In some places, nothing can be left unlocked or unguarded. In other places, a few things can and in still others, the whole plant can be left unlocked 24 hours a day (such as my own parish which, I realize, invites being murdered in my bed some day). The idea is to give the message: this is our property and our common responsibility. Too idealistic, too unsafe? Very likely in most places. At least have as many trusted people with keys as possible. Diffuse the "my plant" attitude.

2. *If you invite and enable shared ministry,* paid or voluntary, you must provide the people with space and place and the means to do their tasks. Among our office spaces we have one empty office marked "Common Office." This is for anyone's use. If people are doing something, even in the most temporary way, they need a phone and a desk. Our common office is both practical and, more importantly, symbolic. Just to see that sign there gives off an important message about the seriousness of collaboration.

3. *A public bulletin board* in the church vestibule for public notices gives a sense of community.

4. *We have fourteen or fifteen enlarged photographs* permanently hanging around the church, some solemn, some full of life and fun, to bespeak a human family at prayer and play.

5. *We have another bulletin board inside the church,* in addition to these permanent enlarged photographs, where every month a whole new set of photographs of parishioners at various functions hang. That always draws an interested crowd.

6. *A guest book* in our vestibule not only enables our community to see who has visited us, but to every legible name and address goes a warm letter of gratitude for coming and the promise of our prayers.

7. *A "Wailing Wall"* (see a fuller explanation in our ministry booklet) tells us all of the needs of others. This is a simulated stone wall we erected in one space in our church (like the "Wailing" or western Wall of Jerusalem). Here people write out their needs, petitions, or whatever is in their hearts and pin them on scraps of paper to the wall. Others are free to come, take the petition and initial it as a sign that they are taking that special need into their own hearts and prayers.

You get the idea. When people walk into the church and immediately see not only the unusual furniture and banners and statues, but the public bulletin board, the permanent and changing photographs of people in action, a wailing wall, a guest book, a common office in the back—the very physical ambiance says human beings live and worship here. The plant, the place, tells of collaboration.

There is one more item here that I can't develop within the scope of this book, only mention. That is, there is such a thing as the aesthetics of spirituality. As much as possible, the buildings and grounds, the decorations and shrubbery, etc., should be in good taste. The whole complex should be pleasing to the eye and heart, be inviting and warm.

The collaboration of subsidiarity. This invites people to be church on the level at which they can operate better than we can. Some practical examples of subsidiarity that promote ownership would be:

1. *Christmas decorating* is a simple thing, but I'm willing to bet that in the average parish the same people have been decorating the church since 1944—and don't anyone dare move a poinsettia. But in our parish, we ask a different neighborhood to decorate each year. True, we take our chances that the results might not be great (they are always), but the point is that whole families, senior citizens, teens, etc., all collaborate to make the church lovely for the holidays. There's a sense of ownership when a teen or child comes to church and tells a friend that he or she put up that Christmas ball on the tree. (We always have a large, fresh tree brought into church each year.) The sense of "ownership," of responsibility, is really marvelous to see. Again, a simple thing, but a fine example of the collaboration of subsidiarity.

2. *Likewise, we have had fifteen families make life-size crosses,* which we erect on the property every Passiontide as a strong reminder to all who pass by on the highway of what is happening. (On Good Friday, rain or shine, we have the outdoor stations with a usual crowd of 1100 to 1300.) Again, the point is that different families made those crosses—as different ones built the outdoor Christmas crib.

3. *Different families are responsible for the grounds and flowers* on different parts of the property. Men and women bake our altar bread, lead the stations of the cross on the Friday evenings of Lent, serve as entire families for our monthly High Mass (complete with robes for all family members), and select the material which each Advent and Lent we mail out to all the families of the parish. People also write one-page reflections for Advent and Lent that are inserted into our Sunday bulletins and form our Telecare group, whose members call every family of the parish during the year. They lead the Monday morning prayer service and the Wednesday morning public Divine Office.

There are other more telling examples. For instance, a system of Sponsor Couples in:

1. *A one-to-one ministry,* where people who have experienced and come through some trauma, via; alcoholism, death of a loved one, divorce, etc; can minister to another in the same situation.

2. *Like-to-like catechesis,* whereby we have people catechize their peers. If we have a prospective senior citizen convert, we have another senior citizen catechize him or her. The same with teens, married, unmarried, etc. When you first approach a parishioner and ask him or her to catechize another, the first reaction is naturally hysteria and protestations that the person is unworthy, unlettered, unable, etc. But you reassure the person, reminding him or her that religion is basically caught not taught, that even if they don't have a degree in theology (which might be a hindrance), good Lord, they've been living it for all these years! Besides, you reassure them by giving them a set of tapes and a book and tell them that all they have to do is listen to the tapes together and try to respond to any questions. In every case without fail, the experience has not only been very positive on all sides, but firm friendships and sponsorships have resulted.

3. *Annulments.* I have a couple who were both married to other people and then, outside the Church, to one another. It took a long time to get their annulments, but we finally did. In gratitude, they have taken on the ministry of helping others to get annulments. They go over the forms, give them guidance, type up their reports, etc., and, of course, they come across as sympathetic and understanding.

There are other areas too numerous to mention in which parishes (pastors) can give practical expression to the principle of subsidiarity. For our purposes, we only point them out, to realize that, in practice, shared and collaborative ministry is possible, that there are some practical translations that every parish can make in one form or another. It is we pastors who have to be convinced of the value of collaborative ministry and get our theology straight in seeing the whole parish community as basically ministerial. It is worth it, for in the process, we will sense a new power and a new meaning in our very old role of presbyter.

Well, as we end this chapter, perhaps we can try to mull over and make our own this formula from an effective southern California pastor of some 4,000 families, a formula that summarizes much of what we have written here. His formula is:

1. I must develop listening skills.
2. I must trust my people.
3. I must be ready to endure the messiness of shared decision making.
4. I must give volunteers and staff people in the parish permission to fail.
5. I must demand that lay leaders serve limited terms.
6. I believe in my own prophetic gifts.
7. Not all good ideas come from out of the diocesan offices.
8. There are no problems, only opportunities.
9. Less control over the parish requires more maturity on my part.
10. I must not stop growing.

The only reason this woman went to church every Sunday was because she was so deeply impressed with the pastor's sermons. "I never get tired of hearing that man preach," she said to her friend. "He's such a wonderful preacher that you would think that every word he said was true!"

This story may be only one notch above the comic strip "Kudzu" in which the character, Preacher Dunn, goes into the pulpit and says to the congregation, "Brothers and sisters, today I want to give you a test—a spiritual test. This test will measure your level of spiritual development as a congregation. Ready? First, complete this sentence: 'Whosoever will strike you on the right cheek...' " Immediately, the cries come from the congregation, "String him up! Waste him!" Then Preacher Dunn says, "I may be forced to grade this on a curve."

John announced to his brother monk that he was
going off to the desert alone to live as an angel.
After several days the monk heard a knock at the
door. "Who is it?" he asked. A voice, weakened by
hunger, replied, "John!" The monk inside re-
sponded, "John, it can't be, for John is an angel
and has no need of food or shelter." But he
relented and took the humbled John in to live a
more incarnational life.

IX

Contexts
of Priestly Spirituality

IN 1984, THE NATIONAL FEDERATION OF PRIESTS' COUNCILS SENT OUT A
"Role of the Pastor" Survey Report, the results of which were
to be relayed to the National Council of Catholic Bishops. The
survey asked six questions. The first and the fourth questions
are of interest to us here. The first question asked, "What are
your most strongly felt convictions about the role of pastor
today?" The survey report: "Two areas stood out in the
response. The first saw the pastor as a person of prayer and
study, one whose spirituality was real and who conveyed that
to the people. Scripture was an important part of their lives,
with a great concern to preach God's word in an effective way.

In a phrase, the pastor is a spiritual leader." Question number four asked for, "The Criteria for Judging a Good and Effective Pastor." The survey report: "The answer which had the largest number of responses said a good and effective pastor was one who had a serious spiritual life, a deep faith, and was prayerful." So priestly spirituality stands out as the best mark of the priest, his most effective characteristic, above all others. Still, what precisely is this priestly spirituality? This may be hard to answer, and I leave the task to others more qualified than I am. Nevertheless, I think we can confidently list five contexts within which the whole question must at least be addressed.

The first context is that of adaptability. The reason for this is obvious. Our priestly culture is no longer an identifiable one: breviary, cassock, biretta (a good trivia question: what is a biretta?), rosary, collar, and rectory. These may or may not be part of the lifestyle of some priests. Moreover, any presumed separate or caste road to holiness has been leveled by Vatican II's clear call to *universal* holiness *(Lumen Gentium, 2)*. This not only means that the priestly or religious life is no longer seen as a privileged or unique way to the kingdom, but that necessarily this narrow preserve of holiness had to expand to include all. The council distinctly focused such "democratic" holiness on the public sacraments, prayer, and liturgy and made the firm point that the main focus of the spiritual life is in the parish and even in the world. Certainly the monastery, convent, or rectory were no longer exclusive centers of spirituality. Prayer and spirituality nowadays are basically public and communal. This has cut the ground from under private devotions and left both clergy and laity somewhat at sea. It has been an especially big adjustment for those of us raised on the monastic model of spirituality or the seminary models of the seventeenth century French school of the Sulpicians and the Vincentians.

The emphasis on liturgy, community, sacraments, and Scripture further undermined support for private non-sacramental practices. . . . The net result of the devaluing and discrediting of older popular devotions in the absence of any concilar reforms. . . is a kind of vacuum in the devotional life of most parish communities and families. . . . [Too bad] for these habits accumulated many of the small details of daily life into a pattern of behavior that linked the person one was in church and sacraments with the person one was in the rest of life. They helped resist the very dichotomy between church and world that the council observed, lamented and sought to redress as its major task. . . . [In any event] two things seem clear. First, the old devotions will not do. Second, their pastoral function may well be indispensible to Catholicism as a way of life; that function must be retrieved, although in some new form.[1]

I agree about the pastoral function of popular devotions that tic in communal with workaday life, as I agree with the need to make adaptations. And this applies to priestly spirituality. We can no longer run on monastic hand-me-downs (if we ever could), but must find ways to be whole and holy. Recognition of the change, of the council's emphasis on corporate life and sacramentality, of the ensuing decline of popular devotions is the groundwork of reassessment and adaptability.

Furthermore, it seems to me that adaptability also includes a moving away from a narrowly clerical in-house spirituality, one that unconsciously confines us only to sanctuary and churchy parameters. By that I mean the common trap that both clergy and laity fall into: of "seeing" God and his grace only in certified places, of portioning off in strict divisions the sacred and the secular much to our impoverishment. We have to move beyond the altar, as it were, to expand to this whole God-filled world:

We practice spiritual exercises or indulge in worship services while we detach ourselves from our bodies and physical surroundings. We keep matters of faith in one room of our life and we spend most of our time in the remaining rooms. We accept a lopsided and limited spirituality, narrowly focused on a one-dimensional God.

Serious consequences follow. Only parts of ourselves are
drawn into prayer and the journey of faith. We leave
behind, with a dogged sense of discipline, our senses,
our imaginations, our creative impulses. We predeter-
mine our places and times of prayer. We freeze our
growth exactly where childhood instruction left
us. . . . We overlook the grace hidden in this practical
event, this particular emotion, this here-and-now of
beauty, pain or compassion. We read only the italics of
our lives and neglect the common, everyday print. We
use a language of the elite and fail to communicate the
deeper dimensions of our lives to those around us. Our
faith is clothed in mystique, our spiritual sharing is ar-
tificial, our vision of holiness becomes abstract and
bloodless and unattractive. We approach life and people as problems. Mysteries are reserved to the Trinity.
We trust computers and calculators but not our own
healthy instincts and holy insights.[2]

Adaptability urges us priests to a wider spiritual vision and
activity than perhaps our clerical training has indicated. Our
"sanctuary," where we feel most at home, has to be expanded
to include this graceful world.

  The second context of priestly spirituality takes adaptability
a step further and says that, if it is to be genuine, it must be
incarnational. I like the old priest's prayer from another era
who used to exclaim heartily, "O Lord, use me, use me—in
some advisory capacity!" Today we are more apt to be in sympathy with the priest who spirituality urges him to be concerned about food for the hungry, because every assualt on
human beings is an attack on Christ, who shared human life.
John carmody puts it this way, "'To teach, heal, engineer, de-
fend at the bar, or make beautivul things in a spirit of justice
and helpfulness is to bend work toward the service of God's
kingdom."[3] Or there's James Fenhagen's insight. "Holiness is
a description of what happens when the experience of God
which is deepened in us in the life of the gathered Church
drives us into the events of day-to-day life with a new perspective."[4] In a word, for priests, as for all, there can be no genuine spirituality unless somehow it spills over into concern
for this incarnational world. Monastic withdrawal or the "man
apart" are not viable options for the secular priest. I think this

is one lesson that Merton left us. Social justice, caring and sharing, and all the rest must find a natural incarnational fallout from our life in the "gathered church."

Because it is not often mentioned, I would like to add to the obvious social justice expressions of incarnational spirituality, the less perceived one of imagination and art. We seldom see either one as powerful factors in holiness, and yet, ironically, our history is replete with both, which have nurtured and nourished many saints. Our Catholic tradition is rich with imagery, so much so, that we are often warned of the danger of spinning off into voodoo and magic, while our Protestant brothers and sisters face the danger of spinning off into a philosophy of religion. But the fact is that the church predates the printed word of the New Testament and, in its better moments, has sought God's presence in all of creation. The church has freely baptized everything from pagan peoples to pagan feasts, such as Christmas.

> The Catholic religious imagination, and the theological systems emerging from it tend to emphasize the similarity between God and objects, events, experiences, and persons in the natural world, while the Protestant (and Islamic and Jewish) religious imaginations and the theologies emerging from them tend to emphasize the difference between God and objects, events, experiences, and persons in the natural world. The tendency of the Catholic imagination is to say "similar" first and the Protestant imagination to say "different" first. The Protestant imagination stresses opposition between God and the World: God is totally other, radically, drastically, and absolutely different from His creation. The Catholic imagination responds by saying that God is similar to the world and has revealed Himself/Herself in the world, especially through the human dimension of Jesus.[5]

We've always been noted for our earthiness and the crafts and arts which celebrate it. And such crafts and arts have been, as we said, nourishing, inviting, and enchanting and, if truth were known, the envy of our Protestant brothers and sisters. I like Nathanial Hawthorne's side glance in *The Scarlet Letter* as he describes Hester and her child: "Had there been a Papist among the crowd of Puritans, he might have seen

in this beautiful woman, so picturesque in her attire and mien
and with the infant at her bosom, an object to remind him
of the image of the Divine Maternity, which so many il-
lustrious painters have vied with one another to represent;
something which should remind him, indeed, but only by contrast, of that sacred image of sinless motherhood, whose infant was to redeem the world."

Or, if you wish, try modern writer Garrison Keillor's side
glance at Catholics:

> Jesus said, "Where two or three are gathered together
> in my name, there am I in the midst of them," and the
> Brethren believed that was enough. We met in Uncle
> Al's and Aunt Flo's bare living room with plain folding
> chairs arranged facing in toward the middle. No
> clergyman in black smock. No organ or piano, for that
> would make one person too prominent. No upholstery,
> it would lead to complacency. No picture of Jesus. He
> was in our hearts.
>
> There was a lovely silence in the Brethren assembled
> on Sunday morning as we waited for the Spirit. . . . It was
> like sitting on the porch with your family, when nobody
> feels that they have to make talk. . . . So peaceful, and
> we loved each other too. I thought perhaps the Spirit was
> leading me to say that, but I was just a boy, and children
> were supposed to keep still. And my affections were not
> pure. They were tainted with a sneaking admiration of
> Catholics—Catholic Christmas, Easter, the Living
> Rosary, and the Blessing of Animals, all magnificent.
> Everything we did was plain, but they were regal and
> gorgeous. . . . "Christians," my Uncle Al used to say, "do
> not go in for show," referring to the Catholics.[6]

Margaret R. Miles in her excellent book *Image As Insight*
reminds us that religion has been frequently described as a
way of seeing. It implies "perceiving a quality of the sensible
world, a numinosity, a 'certain slant of light,' in which other
human beings, the natural world, and objects appear in their
full beauty, transformed. The transient, intensely experienced
occasions on which we experience 'eyesight as insight' have
frequently been described as a clue to the nature and struc-

ture of reality and the first step toward realization of the ultimate fulfillment of human being as symbolized by the idea of the vision of God."[7] She also reminds us that from the beginning of Christianity, the arts have flourished and been accepted as an incarnational means of revealing God. It was a while back too that the noted film critic Pauline Kael remarked how most of the insightful and powerful motion pictures, rich with symbolism and meaning, came from Catholic directors. And what was it that playwright Eugene Ionesco said? "Malraux said that the twenty-first century will be religious or will not be at all. Make it be religious. Art is the human activity that is closest to the spiritual." So, the message is clear: whatever the dangers of magic, our Catholic heritage follows that of the God-Man, and does not disdain the arts; and that, in fact, the arts are an exquisite way of revealing God's presence once again. Perhaps we should let Thomas Merton have the last word here:

> I had learned from my own father that it was almost blasphemy to regard the function of art as merely to reproduce some kind of sensible pleasure or, at best, to stir up the emotions' transitory thrill. I had always understood that art was contemplation, and that it involved the action of the highest faculties....I had understood that the artistic experience, at its highest, was actually a natural analogue of the mystical experience. It produced a kind of intuitive perception of reality through...effective identification with the object contemplated.[8]

Again, all this lengthy discussion is to emphasize that priestly incarnational spirituality must somehow include the arts.

The third context for priestly spirituality is relationships. Boston psychiatrist, Jean Baker-Miller, author of the insightful *Toward a New Psychology of Women*, writes in *Ms.* magazine of a woman doctor who practices in a prestigious Boston hospital and who, in order to get ahead, must master a variety of complicated medical procedures, put her best foot forward in her daily rounds, and convince her superiors that she is smart, willing, and ambitious. The problem is, she originally chose medicine, not because she wanted to dazzle the chiefs of staff, but because she wanted to help patients. But the demands of the field won't allow her to pursue her primary goal. She begins to feel depressed instead of seeing that institutional pressures are to blame for the feelings she has. Dr. Miller tries to help her understand that "winning, looking out for number one" is a destructive model. Then she adds—and here we must attend to her words—"I don't think you can get much real personal satisfaction and fulfillment in life without having close personal relationships. This doesn't mean that you have to get married. It doesn't even mean that you have to have relationships with men. But it does mean that you have to examine whether you are destroying and diminishing relationships rather than enlarging and deepening them." Miller also goes on to argue that from their first years and throughout their lives human beings develop *because of*, not in spite of, others.[9]

Apply this to yourselves. If you're serving the institution rather than people; if, as every priestly survey shows as the number one problem, you are lonely, then you should not be surprised that you perceive no growth in the spiritual life. If you neglect human relationships, your life, your spirituality will be cramped. Notice that Miller says you don't have to be married or have sexual relationships in order to grow, but you do have to have warm and caring and open human relationships if you are to develop as human beings and as a saint. Yet, unlike women, we won't even ask another man to go to the doctor's office with us though we might want badly to have some company there. Even serving others, which we have publicly chosen, is considered in our culture rather low level stuff. Our lives in fact are organized against such, and we have to fight to keep our ideals. Oh, we can easily serve other "lesser beings," such as women and children; but seldom can we serve our "equals," other men, at least directly, since our relationship to them is competitive, and we must strive for power over them. To ask for help, that most fundamental trusting and vulnerable relationship—that has been conditioned out of us, for to show need is to be considered somehow less of a man.

Robert Weiss, writing in the magazine *Family Process*, says pretty much the same thing, "It has been shown repeatedly that although stressful life situations foster distress and illness, individuals who can rely on the support of others are less vulnerable than those who cannot."[10] Yet, like most American males surveyed, priests can count many acquaintances but few if any close friends. This fact alone may be the most telling barometer of our spiritual life.

The fourth context for a healthy spiritual life is as public as it is brief, namely, recreation. It's the old "healthy mind in a healthy body" axiom. Some physical and psychical exercise, just some plain fun and relaxing, is absolutely mandatory especially for workaholic-prone people like priests. The problem is that no one checks up on us: no wife (which is why married men live longer and are healthier than single men), no bishop and often no confrere. We must work out some kind of buddy system to ensure that we take care of this context.

The fifth and final context for a healthy priestly spirituality is coming to terms with our sexuality. There's an interesting article I would like to share here from Episcopal priest, James B. Nelson.[11] Nelson identifies three issues that connect male spirituality and sexuality, issues that need to be looked at and come to terms with: the genitalization of sex, homophobia, and the fear of death. You don't have to agree with all of his points, but they are worth pondering.

The genitalization of sex means that boys and men tend to isolate sex from other areas of life. (We see this most grossly in rapid anonymous homo- and heterosexual sexual encounters.) They find the genitals very important to their self-image since they are obviously external, visible, accessible to excited touch, pleasure, and masturbation. Undersized genitals, although perfectly capable of functioning well, are an embarrassment for males. Bigger is better. More frequent intercourse is a sign of a healthy stud. Hugh Hefner who in his biography is said to have impregnated over 2000 women is the sexual hero. All this reinforces the attitude that sexual feelings are totally in the genitals rather than diffused throughout one's whole body and soul. Therefore, the male expression of sex is discovered in the external act which is, of course, obvious, and therefore, external performance is important with little energy left over for meaning.

The woman, on the other hand, tends to find sex a more internal and mysterious reality. The male tends to experience his body, his genitals, more as an instrument of penetrating and exploring a mystery outside of and external to itself. To this extent, mystery is to be conquered and controlled. It is no wonder, then, that male spirituality is geared to penetrating mystery without rather than embracing it within. No wonder we project our sexuality onto God and evolve a church with its penchant for law, order, and rationality (control). No wonder we tend to accentuate the act and the performance (build any buildings lately?) as opposed to relationship and meaning (build any community lately?). It may be, then, that any trouble we are having with celibacy is not due to too much relationship, but to too little.

Intimacy, by the way, comes harder for us males than for the females, because, unlike the girls who from the start experience themselves *like* their mothers and so find their gender natural, we males experience ourselves from the start as being *opposite* from our mothers and so we define ourselves by separation. Notice the old negative phrases from our childhood: "I am not a girl! I am not a sissy! I don't cry! I don't run to mommy when I'm hurt!, etc. . . . " So it winds up that intimacy threatens our male sense of gender since we have been established from the beginning in terms of separation from the female. Now you know why we resonate with Shane riding off into the sunset with his foster son crying after him or why the cowboy is fonder of his horse than his girlfriend.

Homophobia is another sexual stumbling block to a healthy spirituality. Homophobia is the irrational fear of the same-sex attraction and affection. The gay male threatens the straight male because he is able to be submissive in the sexual or non-sexual male relationship which the straight male would like to be but can't. The gay male further symbolizes male-to-male acceptance, tenderness, and intimacy – all of which the straight male lacks. This commentary is not meant as endorsement, merely an insight. Therefore, as you can see, homophobia restricts men to the buddy system and prevents really deep friendships. Again, is this why survey after survey does show men of all walks of life and age with few or no close male friends? This fear naturally limits men's interests. They may, in fact, be lonely in the best sense for other men but don't know how to express it without the spectre of homosexuality. No Jonathans for us Davids.

So, we don't know how to deal with other men openly and vulnerably, which may be why (1) we go the route of competition, and (2) horse around and slap and punch – all distancing gestures. Is it any wonder we have no theology of friendship since heretofore most theologians were men? And do our relations with men not spill over to our relations to a very masculine God? True, Jesus presents us with a God who as a father hugs another male in the Prodigal Son story, but we can't adopt that image for ourselves. We have in the past compensated by producing the cult of the Virgin, but that's been in decline lately. So it leaves us men with no other outlets, deepens our loneliness, and affects our celibate spirituality.

Death is related to sexuality because we all experience "little deaths" in our erections. Death is the final defeat of hardness and performance. We know its power but also its continual loss. In one sense, all males are defeated in intercourse. While she can go on endlessly, he deflates. Death is the final deflation, the final challenge to linear, external thought, action, control, and winning. If men are dedicated to these by their sexual self-understanding, then death is truly the

ultimate defeat and fear. Accordingly, by and large, men fear
death more than women, who act and perceive more
cyclically.

Without denying the marvelous sensations of our genital
sexual energy, we must find a better balance in the interest
of our spirituality. We have to learn to diffuse our sexual feelings. This means a great measure of self-acceptance of our
bodies, of our aesthetic side, of imagination, of the world.
We must learn that we are body, we are graced, that we can
have warm relationships as celibates, that we can express our
tenderness. We do not have to achieve, penetrate, or capture
the mystery. Even our homophobia can be overcome by learning to love the whole body-self that each of us is – including
the homoerotic desires that are a natural part of all men.
Perhaps someday someone will do us a favor and provide us
with a theology of erotic feelings and friendship. This would
improve our priestly spirituality immensely.

So, there are our five contexts for a consideration of priestly
spirituality: adaptability, incarnational, relationships, recreation, and sexuality. The trick, as always, is to translate these
concepts into practice. For this I suggest that we have to turn
to the spiritual masters among us. Meanwhile, on the practical level, I can share some areas that may be helpful in moving us in the right direction.

First of all, since we are secular priests – men of and in
the world – the monastic model of spirituality simply doesn't
work for us, if for no other reason than we never can count
on defined and planned time. Besides, should we relate to
and pray only with other priests and religious? It seems to
me that a vital part of our particular spiritual development
must come from the very people we serve. We must not only
pray *for* our people but also *with* them. Our celibacy frees
us to be with them. Should we not, therefore, also draw
nourishment from them and share with them?

I can mention four practical instances I have found helpful
in doing so as a parish priest. About half a dozen years ago,
perceiving the real hungering for prayer among the people,

I realized that they did not have too many formal ways to satisfy that hunger. So I sent personal letters to about thirty men asking if they would be interested in learning how to chant the Divine Office. About twenty responded. We got together, learned the mechanics, meaning, and genius behind the office, and then started using the *Catholic Worship Book*. Our routine was to meet at 6:30 in the morning, before commuting time, in our spiritual center chapel. The format, which lasted about 20 minutes to a half hour consisted of an opening hymn, prayer, chanting of the psalm, short Scripture reading and reflection, the Benedictus, the Our Father, communion, meditation time, prayers of the faithful, and a closing prayer and hymn. Those who could stay for coffee and donuts were welcomed to do so. I was not prepared for both the enthusiasm and the perseverance. Our numbers have swelled to about fifty men divided between two mornings a week. The women, seeing the impact on the men, have started to meet on another morning.

The point is that over the years I have learned to enjoy praying *with* the men and have found great support and fellowship in their company, as well as nourishment from them when they take turns leading the morning office. Their approach, homilies, concerns, prayer spill over and enrich me. I feel as if I am living a parish-people spirituality rather than a monastic one. Second, I have had the same experience in the renew group I am in. Third, I have always encouraged the people (especially since the specter of the priest shortage has become more real) to learn how to lead public and devotional prayer. In our parish lay people will lead the Novena, the Stations of the Cross, and on occasion give the weekend homily, lead our Monday morning prayer service, wake services, and Scripture-sharing groups. Being among them as a participant, rather than always as a leader, moves my own prayer life into their concerns and lives.

Fourth and finally, given that prayer hunger, I have promoted within the parish itself a forum for spiritual direction. A Sister associate pastor showed promise here, and so the parish sent her away for three summers to Creighton University, where she earned her masters in spiritual direction. Under continuing professional supervision she has been on the property to offer truly in-depth spiritual direction for our people, both singly and in groups. As their spiritual and prayer lives grow so do they, in many silent ways, influence and upgrade the rest of us. The priest or religious are not the only ones with the luxury of spiritual direction. Now we can all share in its promise. Once more, this adaptability has at least given me some movement away from an exclusively clerical approach to the spiritual life. It has broadened me into greater participation with and support from our common journey with the people.

Many dioceses have introduced priest support groups such as Emmaus, and this has been good. Such programs bring us together for, like lawyers or doctors or engineers, there are rhythms peculiar to us that only a gathered camaraderie can expose and explore. Spiritual direction, confession, and retreats are still, of course, solid staples in the formulas of our spiritual development. But there are two other items that may be not only overlooked but downplayed and which are in fact, I believe, necessary expressions of our five contexts for a priestly spiritual life. These items are the twins of study and sabbatical. The fact is, that because we are guilty victims of a false spirituality which makes us slaves to schedules, activism, and overwork, we really do not take time – haven't the time – to study, beyond a glance at a clerical magazine or an occasional pious book. As a result, our intellectual life contracts, our vision of life narrows, our spiritual vitality dries up or becomes excessively clerical, and our homilies suffer. We must keep abreast, read, take a few courses here and there, whatever. And, it has been my experience and that of others, that usually we have to get off the property to do this.

So, to paraphrase Hamlet, get thee to a hideaway with thy book; take mini-courses at nearby colleges, attend workshops, and don't confine yourself exclusively to clerical or churchy subjects. A good college course on the novel might do more to enrich your theology than twenty-five lectures on Nestorianism. Flaubert or Graham Greene have probably raised more theological issues than Tanquerey.

The Jewish tradition, as you know, is firm on linking study and sanctity. For the Jews, the scholar and the saint are one. "No table is blessed if there is not a scholar to eat at it" is one of their sayings. An ignorant man, they claim, cannot really be pious. That's why Tevye in *Fiddler on the Roof* really wants to be rich: so he can have the leisure to spend seven hours a day discussing the Holy Books with the Wise Men! So not for the Jews is the simple Breton peasant the hero. They are more in sympathy with the great St. Theresa, who preferred a smart confessor to a holy, but dumb one. We must take a page from this tradition and once more connect study with spirituality. The cousin to this admonition is to hold in high esteem that protracted study we call the sabbatical. There is no question in my mind that every priest, at least every seven years, or especially at normal assignment change time, should take a sabbatical, however brief. Stepping back, so to speak, is not only good for the soul, but also for morale and growth. I think Bishop Sullivan of Richmond has made sabbaticals mandatory. This likely will be, I suspect, a short-term hardship, but certainly a long-term gain all the way around. Routine, expected (by both priests and laity), legitimized clerical sabbaticals are a sensible and practical means of spiritual development. They have the potential to catch effectively all of the five contexts we described for a rounded priestly spiritual life.

At this point we usually tack on a little story for relief. In this present context our addition will be a whole chapter unto itself: Thomas Hardy's delightful *Old Mrs. Chundle*. It's not only a charming and humorous story, but also one that ultimately draws us into its power, because, in many ways, it is our story.

X

"Old Mrs. Chundle"

Thomas Hardy

THE CURATE HAD NOT BEEN A WEEK IN THE PARISH, BUT THE AUTUMN morning proving fine, he thought he would make a little water-colour sketch, showing a distant view of the Corvsgate ruin two miles off, which he had passed on his way hither. The sketch occupied him a longer time than he had anticipated. The luncheon hour drew on, and he felt hungry.

Quite near him was a stone-built old cottage of respectable and substantial build. He entered it, and was received by an old woman.

"Can you give me something for lunch?" he shouted. "Bread and cheese-anything will do."

A sour look crossed her face, and she shook her head. "That's unlucky," murmured he. She reflected and said more urbanely, "Well, I'm going to have my own bit o' dinner in no such long time hence. 'Tis taters and cabbage, boiled with a scantling o' bacon. Would ye like it? But I suppose 'tis the wrong sort, and that ye would sooner have bread and cheese."

"No, I'll join you. Call me when it is ready. I'm just out here."

"Aye, I've seen ye. Drawing old stones, bain't ye?"

"Yes, my good woman."

"Sure 'tis well some folk have nothing better to do with their time. Very well, I'll call ye, when I've dished up."

He went out and resumed his painting; till in about seven or ten minutes the old woman appeared at her door and held up her hand. The curate washed his brush, went to the brook, rinsed his hands and proceeded to the house.

"There's yours," she said, pointing to the table. "I'll have my bit here." And she denoted the settle.

"Why not join me?"

"Oh, faith, I don't want to eat with my betters – not I." And she continued firm in her resolution, and ate apart.

The vegetables had been well cooked over a wood fire – the only way to cook a vegetable properly – and the bacon was well boiled. The curate ate heartily: he thought he had never tasted such potatoes and cabbage in his life, which he probably had not, for they had been just brought in from the garden, so that the very freshness of the morning was still in them. When he had finished he asked her how much he owed for the repast, which he had much enjoyed.

"Oh, I don't want to be paid for that bit of snack 'a believe!"

"But really you must take something. It was an excellent meal."

"'Tis all my own growing, that's true. But I don't take money for a bit o' victuals. I've never done such a thing in my life."

"I would feel much happier if you would."

She seemed unsettled by his feeling, and added as by compulsion, "Well, then; I suppose twopence won't hurt ye?"

"Twopence?"

"Yes. Twopence."

"Why my good woman, that's no charge at all. I am sure it is worth this at least." And he laid down a shilling.

"I tell 'ee 'tis *twopence*, and no more!" she said primly. "Why, bless the man, it didn't cost me more than three halfpence, and that leaves me a fair quarter profit. The bacon is the heaviest item; that may perhaps be a penny. The taters I've got plenty of, and the cabbage is going to waste."

He thereupon argued no further, paid the limited sum demanded, and went to the door. "And where does that road lead?" he asked, by way of engaging her in a friendly conversation before parting, and pointing to a white lane which branched from the direct highway near her door.

"They tell me that it leads to Enckworth."

"And how far is Enckworth?"

"Three miles, they say. But God knows if 'tis true."

"You haven't lived here long, then?"

"Five-and-thirty year come Martinmas."

"And yet you have never been to Enckworth?"

"Not I. Why should I ever have been to Enckworth? I never had any business there—a great mansion of a place, holding people that I've no more doings with than with the people of the moon. No, there's on'y two places I ever go to from year's end to year's end: that's once a fortnight to Anglebury, to do my bit o' marketing, and once a week to my parish church."

"Which is that?"

"Why, Kingscreech."

"Oh—then you are in my parish?"

"Maybe. Just on the Outskirts."

"I didn't know the parish extended so far. I'm a newcomer. Well, I hope we may meet again. Good afternoon to you."

When the curate was next talking to his rector he casually observed: "By the way, that's a curious old soul who lives out towards Corvsgate—old Mrs.—I don't know her name—a deaf old woman."

"You mean old Mrs. Chundle, I suppose."

"She tells me she's lived there five-and-thirty years, and has never been to Enckworth, three miles off. She goes to two places only, from year's end to year's end—to the market town, and to church on Sundays."

"To church on Sundays. H'm. She rather exaggerates her

travels, to my thinking. I've been rector here thirteen years, and I have certainly never seen her at church in my time."

"A wicked old woman. What can she think of herself for such deception!"

"She didn't know you belonged here when she said it, and could find out the untruth of her story. I warrant she wouldn't have said it to me!" And the rector chuckled.

On reflection the curate felt that this was decidedly a case for his ministrations, and on the first spare morning he strode across to the cottage beyond the ruin. He found its occupant of course at home.

"Drawing picters again?" she asked, looking up from the hearth, where she was scouring the fire-dogs.

"No, I come on a more important matter, Mrs. Chundle, I am the new curate of this parish."

"You said you was last time. And after you had told me and went away I said to myself he'll be here again sure enough, hang me if I didn't. And here you be."

"Yes. I hope you don't mind?"

"Oh, no. You find us a roughish lot, I make no doubt?"

"Well, I won't go into that. But I think it was a very culpable – unkind thing of you to tell me you came to church every Sunday, when I find you've not been seen there for years."

"Oh, did I tell 'ee that?"

"You certainly did."

"Now I wonder what I did that for?"

"I wonder too."

"Well, you could ha' guessed, after all, that I didn't come to any service. Lord, what's the good o' my lumpering all the way to church and back again, when I'm as deaf as a plock? Your own common sense ought to have told 'ee that 'twas but a figure o' speech, seeing you was a pa'son."

"I'm sure I couldn't. Oh no – not a word. Why I couldn't hear anything even at that time when Isaac Coggs used to cry the Amens out loud beyond anything that's done nowadays, and they had the barrel-organ for the tunes – years and years agone, when I was stronger in my narves than now."

"H'm—I'm sorry. There's one thing I could do, which I would with pleasure, if you'll use it. I could get you an ear-trumpet. Will you use it?"

"Ay, sure. That I woll. I don't care what I use—'tis all the same to me."

"And you'll come?"

"Yes. I may as well go there as bide here, I suppose."

The ear-trumpet was purchased by the zealous young man, and the next Sunday, to the great surprise of the parishioners when they arrived, Mrs. Chundle was discovered in the front seat of the nave of Kingscreech Church, facing the rest of the congregation with an unmoved countenance.

She was the centre of observation through the whole morning service. The trumpet, elevated at a high angle, shone and flashed in the sitters' eyes as the chief object in the sacred edifice.

The curate could not speak to her that morning, and called the next day to inquire the result of the experiment. As soon as she saw him in the distance she began shaking her head.

"No, no." she said decisively as he approached. "I knowed 'twas all nonsense."

"What?"

"'Twasn't a mossel o' good, and so I could have told 'ee before. A-wasting your money in jimcracks upon a' old 'ooman like me."

"You couldn't hear? Dear me—how disappointing."

"You might as well have been mouthing at me from the top o' Creech Barrow."

"That's unfortunate."

"I shall never come no more—never—to be made such a fool of as that again."

The curate mused. "I'll tell you what, Mrs. Chundle. There's one thing more to try, and only one. If that fails I suppose we shall have to give it up. It is a plan I have heard of, though I have never myself tried it; it's having a sound tube fixed, with its lower mouth in the seat immediately below the pulpit, where you would sit, the tube running up inside the pulpit with its upper end opening in a bell-mouth just beside the book-board. The voice of the preacher enters the bell-mouth, and is carried down directly to the listener's ear. Do you understand?"

"Exactly."

"And you'll come, if I put it up at my own expense?"

"Ay, I suppose, I'll try it, e'en though I said I wouldn't. I may as well do that as do nothing, I reckon."

The kind-hearted curate, at great trouble to himself, obtained the tube and had it fixed vertically as described, the upper mouth being immediately under the face of whomever should preach, and on the following Sunday morning it was to be tried. As soon as he came from the vestry the curate perceived to his satisfaction Mrs. Chundle in the seat beneath, erect and at attention, her head close to the lower orifice of the second-pipe, and look of great complacency that her soul required a special machinery to save it, while other people's could be saved in a commonplace way. The rector read the prayers from the desk on the opposite side, which parts of the service Mrs. Chundle could follow easily enough by the help of the prayer-book; and in due course the curate mounted the eight steps into the wooden octagon, gave out his text, and began to deliver his discourse.

It was a fine frosty morning in early winter, and he had not got far with his sermon when he became conscious of a steam rising from the bellmouth of the tube, obviously caused by Mrs. Chundle's breathing at the lower end, and it was accompanied by a suggestion of onion-stew. However, he preached on a while, hoping it would cease, holding in his left hand his finest cambric handkerchief kept especially for Sunday morning services. At length, no longer able to endure the odour, he lightly dropped the handkerchief into the bell of the tube, without stopping a moment the eloquent flow of his words; and he had the satisfaction of feeling himself in comparatively pure air.

He heard a fidgeting below; and presently there arose to

him over the pulpit-edge a hoarse whisper: "The pipe's chokt!"

"Now, as you will perceive, my brethren," continued the curate, unheeding the interruption; "by applying this test to ourselves, our discernment of. . . ."

"The pipe's chokt!" came up in a whisper yet louder and hoarser.

"Our discernment of actions as morally good or indifferent will be much quickened, and we shall be materially helped in our. . . ."

Suddenly came a violent puff of warm wind, and he beheld his handkerchief rising from the bell of the tube and floating to the pulpit floor. The little boys in the gallery laughed, thinking it a miracle. Mrs. Chundle had, in fact, applied her mouth to the bottom end, blown with all her might, and cleared the tube. In a few seconds the atmosphere of the pulpit became as before, to the curate's great discomfiture. Yet stop the orifice again he dared not, lest the old woman should make a still greater disturbance and draw the attention of the congregation to this unseemly situation.

"If you carefully analyze the passage I have quoted," he continued in somewhat uncomfortable accents, "you will perceive that it naturally suggests three points for consideration. . . ."

("It's not onions; it's peppermint," he said to himself.)

"Namely, mankind in its unregenerate state. . . ."

("And cider.")

"The incidence of the law, and loving-kindness or grace, which we will now severally consider. . . ."

("And pickled cabbage. What a terrible supper she must have made.")

"Under the twofold aspect of external and internal consciousness."

Thus the reverend gentleman continued strenuously for perhaps five minutes longer; then he could stand it no more. Desperately thrusting his thumb into the hole, he drew the threads of his distracted discourse together, the while hearing her blow vigorously to dislodge the plug. But he stuck to the hole, and brought his sermon to a premature close.

He did not call on Mrs. Chundle the next week, a slight cooling of his zeal for spiritual welfare being manifest; but he encountered her at the house of another cottager whom he was visiting; and she immediately addressed him as a partner in the same enterprise.

"I could hear beautiful!" she said. "Yes; every word! Never did I know such a wonderful machine as that there pipe. But you forgot what you was doing once or twice, and put your handkerchief on the top o'en, and stopped the sound a bit. Please not to do that again, for it makes me lose a lot. Howsomever, I shall come every Sunday morning reg'lar now, please God."

The curate quivered internally.

"And will ye come to my house once in a while and read to me?"

"Of course."

Surely enough the next Sunday the ordeal was repeated for him. In the evening he told his trouble to the rector. The rector chuckled.

"You've brought it upon yourself," he said. "You don't know this parish as well as I. You should have left the old woman alone."

"I suppose I should!"

"Thank Heaven, she thinks nothing of my sermons, and doesn't come when I preach. Ha, ha!"

"Well," said the curate somewhat ruffled, "I must do something. I cannot stand this. I shall tell her not to come."

"You can hardly do that."

"And I've promised to go and read to her. But—I shan't go."

"She's probably forgotten by this time that you promised."

A vision of his next Sunday in the pulpit loomed horridly before the young man, and at length he determined to escape the experience. The pipe should be taken down. The next morning he gave directions, and the removal was carried out.

A day or two later a message arrived from her, saying that she wished to see him. Anticipating a terrific attack from the irate old woman, he put off going to her for a day, and when he trudged out towards her house on the following afternoon it was in a vexed mood. Delicately nurtured man as he was, he had determined not to re-erect the tube, and hoped he might hit on some new *modus vivendi*, even if any inconvenience to Mrs. Chundle, in a situation that had become intolerable as it was last week.

"Thank Heaven, the tube is gone," he said to himself as he walked; "and nothing will make me put it up again!"

On coming near he saw to his surprise that the calico curtains of the cottage windows were all drawn. He went up to the door, which was ajar; and a little girl peeped through the opening.

"How is Mrs. Chundle?" he asked blandly.

"She's dead, sir," said the girl in a whisper.

"Dead?...Mrs. Chundle dead?"

"Yes, sir."

A woman now came. "Yes, 'tis so, sir. She went off quite sudden-like about two hours ago. Well, you see, sir, she was over seventy years of age, and last Sunday she was rather late in starting for church, having to put her bit o' dinner ready before going out; and was very anxious to be in time. So she hurried overmuch, and runned up the hill, which at her time of life she ought not to have done. It upset her heart, and she's been poorly all the week since, and that made her send for 'ee. Two or three times she said she hoped you would come soon, as you'd promised to, and you were so staunch and faithful in wishing to do her good, that she knew 'twas not by your own wish you didn't arrive. But she would not let us send again, as it might trouble 'ee too much, and there might be other poor folks needing you. She worried to think she might not be able to listen to 'ee next Sunday, and feared you'd be hurt at it, and think her remiss. But she was eager to hear you again later on. However, 'twas ordained otherwise for the poor soul, and was soon gone. I've found a real friend at last,' she said. 'He's a man in a thousand. He's not ashamed of a' old woman, and he holds that her soul is worth saving as well as richer people's.' She said I was to give you this."

It was a small folded piece of paper, directed to him and sealed with a thimble. On opening it he found it to be what she called her will, in which she had left him her bureau, case-clock, four-post bedstead, and framed sampler—in fact all the furniture of any account that she possessed.

The curate went out, like Peter at cock-crow. He was a meek young man, and as he went his eyes were wet. When he reached a lonely place in the lane he stood still thinking, and kneeling down in the dust of the road, rested his elbow in one hand and covered his face with the other.

Thus he remained some minutes or so, a black shape on the hot white of the sunned trackway; till he rose, brushed the knees of his trousers, and walked on.

Father O'Sullivan was visiting sick Mrs. O'Malley. After a few pleasantries he volunteered to say a prayer and read from the family Bible. Mrs. O'Malley piously called to her little daughter in the kitchen: "Honey, bring in that big book that mommy loves and reads so much." In no time the little one came running in with the Sears Roebuck catalog.

XI

Time, Space, Place, and Being Pastoral

JOHN WESLEY ROSE EVERY MORNING AT 5:00 A.M. TO PRAY. SOUNDS both noble and confronting: why can't we do the same? Well, a little reflection reminds us that Wesley, for one thing, lived in the days before electricity so he went to bed soon after dark, say, around 7:30 in the winter. You and I are just beginning our series of evening appointments and meetings around that time. We'd get up at 5:00 a.m. too if we got to bed early. But we never do. There's not enough time.

Time, as the poet Leigh Hunt described it, is a thief. It steals everything away and the lack of it is a chronic clerical complaint. Sometimes priests who retire or change ministries

148

exclaim, "I feel like I'm out of prison. I'm free at last to do the things I ought to do." There's something wrong here when they have to leave their assignment in order to find time to be good priests. But we all know what they mean. Furthermore, with such time pressures come the well-known stress or burnout. Psychiatrist Bruce Baldwin describes personal burnout as "a syndrome resulting from an emotionally destructive relationship to work (or to a career) in which a progressive loss of control, the deterioration of non-work interests, and mixed symptoms reflecting overload and depression result in decreased productivity and general life dissatisfaction." Read that slowly once more and you and I can name dozens of people who fit that description.

Part of our stress from not enough time comes from the fact, as we have seen before, of an increased workload. More has been added to us without any of the old being subtracted. Second, we are fewer in number and, therefore, there is more work for the rest of us to do. Third, we are saddled with unreasonable expectations (a) from the people (b) from the diocese, and (c) from ourselves. These unreasonable expectations range all the way from the imperative that we should do all tasks, read all books, attend every course, visit every sick person, repair every broken window, write out every check, arbitrate every marital discord, and accommodate every church cluster of initials to the ideal hours we should spend in homily preparation, praying, and attending endless meetings. Of course, during all of this we should maintain perfect emotional and physical health and be available for the routinely unexpected. I think what really crunches us all is the real lack of any consensus about priorities in all this. Surveys show that clergy work about 60 to 70 hours a week and the work is never finished. Listen to this one: A 1980 Gallup poll found that 82 percent of clergy considered social action very important or fairly important to their ministry, yet only 8 percent of them said that they actually gave priority to social action. Reason? Not enough time.

Here's another example: Speaking of Bishop Frank Murphy of Baltimore, Fr. Joe Gallagher writes in his book, *The Pain and the Promise:* "Frank's master gift is his chief problem: he's pastoral, personable, and wants to be available. So everyone is after him and he has to fight for breathing space. Very few people, I think, have a grasp of the draining demands made on a pastoral priest or bishop during these years of upheaval and challenge. The danger is that such shepherds will be worn down too soon by the very openness which is so promising."[1] Amen to that!

Father Brian Joyce of California gives some gutsy advice on how to handle time pressures.[2] First, he says, buy a large wastebasket and learn how to throw things away. You simply have to make prudent judgments about your priorities and just what you can reasonably do in a given day, week, or career. Follow your first instincts and toss the others away. Second, learn to delegate. Third, learn to focus; that is, what's your goal or theme for the year in the parish? Try to bend things to that and put all else on the back burner. Finally, I would add, get yourself a buddy like they do in A.A. When you're getting near the frustration point or see it coming in someone else, call, or better, kidnap that person, for some R & R, however brief, somewhere.

I would go further and say that every priest should have some public policy of "planned neglect" of the parish. He should announce to sundry and all that he will be away (or at least not available) two days a week: one day for recreation and the other for prayer and study. It further seems to me that the bishop should make some similar public statement at every pastor's installation. "Father Jim O'Brien is a good priest and we want to use and preserve his talents. He is hereby commanded—and I call upon you people as witness—he is hereby commanded to be dedicated to the planned neglect of this parish. He has a people here who know how to be church without him here all the time. He must take his two days off a week, take his vacation, and his sabbaticals. Any failure on his part to do this is, I remind you, a serious breach of contract, an injustice to you and the gospel and to me. Such failures should be reported directly to me or to the Vicar of Priests!" Oh, for the day we hear those words!

Concerning time-pressure and burnout I have always thought that we Catholics neglect one resource that could be most helpful both on the personal and the parish level: the use of consultants. For some reason—perhaps our clerical Marlboro Man syndrome or the lack of diocesan vision and leadership—we hesitate to seek out consulters. Protestant denominations use them freely and effectively, as does business. There are well-tuned principles on group and organization dynamics. Experienced consulters do come with a fresh perspective and know-how. Often they can move us off dead center and offer some sound recommendations. I would think that a diocese would retain a group of professional consultants to assist individuals or parishes. On the personal level, how would we suspect we might benefit from consultation? These five questions may give us a clue:

1. Do I feel as though my efforts are not as productive, effective, and meaningful as they could be?

2. Is it difficult for me to trust my feelings, intuitions, and decisions in my pastoral role?

3. Do I feel the demand to do more than I am capable of doing?

4. Do I value myself as much as I value those to whom I minister? To what extent is my sense of well-being dependent upon affirmation from others?

5. In what ways am I being ministered to? Who is *my* pastor?

Among the responses to these questions might be the following: (1) time away, (2) friends for relaxation, (3) colleagues for support and encouragement, (4) conferences and workshops for stimulation, (5) professional counseling where indicated, and (6) worship—in the pew for awhile as an average parishioner to get another perspective.

That fifth recommendation speaks of professional counseling. This may simply consist of a short exchange with a clinical psychologist and does not imply anything about one's emotional or mental stability. It's just that at times we all need help or an objective listener. The trouble is that we fear being found out. Even if the diocese is willing to pick up the tab under its insurance plan, you can never be sure of the degree of confidentiality in many chancery offices. None of us likes to be found hurting either by the chancery, the people, or our colleagues. As one pastor put it, "I need help in asking for help."

One creative "in-between" step that some dioceses have inaugurated is having a Vicar for Priests. This is someone not on the Personnel Board but who has direct communication with the bishop, who may ask no questions except to receive recommendations. This gives a trust level for those who want to sound off to an official but who need in that official a confidential and certified friend who transcends diocesan politics. I think of Father Frank McNulty of the Newark, N.J. Archdiocese and the marvelous work he has done in this capacity.

Sometimes the pressures of time are aggravated by our lifestyle and where and how we live (space and place). For years now our model of living has been "over the store." Outside of mothers, we're the only ones I know of who live and work within the same walls twenty-four hours a day. Even when we're relaxing we're on the spot. There's no way to escape detection when you're pooped, outside of dressing up in drag and pretending you're the housekeeper. (The bishop might take a dim view of that.) Then you can add five more possible tensions which may come from living in a rectory, which (1) is very institutional looking and reminds you of either some impersonal corporate office or Sing-Sing; or (2) which is decidedly "owned" by the pastor and you are, at his whim, a guest there; or (3) worse, you must live with his mother or the housekeeper (sometimes they're the same) in a role compared to which Cinderella is a liberated woman; or (4) which houses priests who were, like yourself, just dumped there and with whom you may not be compatible; or (5) which houses your office in which everybody feels free to come and go; in short, you have no privacy.

I think these days, given our needs, numbers, and marketability, we can come to terms with such things a little bit more creatively. Some priests, for example, have opted to live in apartments. Fine, but I think there are other options, options derived from a personal experience I would like to share. About twenty years ago I was assigned to a new parish in Holmdel, N.J., with pastor Bill Anderson. The founding pastor, who had just died, had built a church-school combination. The living situation, however, was difficult. There were two very old farm houses on the property. They were very small and could not accommodate two people in one house so Bill took one house and I the other. Mine was a broken down affair whose core was about 150 years old with hardly any heat, one back entrance (because a sunken floor blocked the front entrance), and a roof that leaked to such an extent that in any rain I had to turn and position my bed to avoid the rain drops and put out a dozen pails to catch them. I loved that old house and both Bill and I eventually got to enjoy the experience of living separately.

Within about two years two things happened: Bill's house caught fire and the local township condemned my house as unfit for human habitation (thanks a lot). So we had to rebuild. We decided to rebuild two small houses instead of one large institutional rectory. We were not prepared then for the people's opposition, who had a very hard time conceiving their priests not living together in a common rectory. It was too strange and novel to them. Still, we went ahead, built two small houses for less than the cost of one large rectory, and proceeded to enjoy each other as well as our independence as secular parish priests.

Anyway, from this experience I have derived this fantasy that from now on parishes should not build large institutional rectories but something on the model of a townhouse or motel. Build separate units with an accessible common room with separate entrances and a little kitchenette. As more priests are (unlikely) added to the staff, merely add another "motel" unit around a common courtyard. This has the benefit of grouping the clergy together, yet at the same time giving them individual privacy and independence. I want, however, to add an important footnote to these suggestions. I spoke of an accessible common room in order to take the edge off too much individualism and doing your own thing. One other "common room," I am convinced, should be included and that is a small Blessed Sacrament chapel. I have often suggested (along with plans!) that as my people's homes grew empty as the children moved out that they should make one room a "meditation" room, complete with pillows on the floor and a focal point such as an icon or crucifix or the Bible. This, I admit, has met with little success. Still, undaunted, I would like to suggest the same for priests. A little common chapel, regardless of living style, would provide a symbolic invitation for busy priests to slow down and offer them a natural place to come together for common prayer. A Blessed Sacrament chapel could be a powerful stimulus to faith and fellowship.

Another thing I learned from my early two-house experience is that since our houses were so small, we had to move the offices over into the school-church complex. We took some storage rooms and made them the parish offices. This too turned out to be a marvelous boon. Now all the offices with their everyday trafficking were out of our houses. So were the secretaries and other staff members. This left your own home for counseling, study, and just living. So freeing was this experience that when I became pastor myself and inherited an already planned, but not yet built, rectory, I was able to persuade the builder to make it like a normal house with no offices but my own. I have moved the offices over to the parish hall (once again, old storage rooms) and continue to enjoy a more normal living pattern.

The moral, I guess, is that we should not raise up any more rectories modeled on the monastery. They make no sense in the light of the priest shortage for one thing. They make no sense for anyone trying to cope with the pressures of time and human living. Not when apartments or regular houses or the like can clone themselves into an attractive pattern for added staff and are more humane, and possibly more emotionally and spiritually healthy. Not to mention that, as times change, you have a more saleable building.

Finally, there is the question of loneliness whether we live communally or separately. As we mentioned before, loneliness ranks high on the clergy list of anxiety, especially these lean days when many pastors, formerly housed with an associate or two, find themselves living alone. At times we can hack it, at other times we can't and to admit this is at least a step in the right direction. And the people know it. Here's a card I received last Christmas from a perceptive lady who's known some hard knocks in life: "Dear Father, My Christmas wish is to express thanks to you for the daily guidance and care you show to every one of us. It must frequently be hard to give of yourself so generously. Most of us have loved ones, as well as the Lord, to lean on in times of need. How lonely it must be when you who must be strong for others cannot share your own weaknesses. May you be blessed for sharing in the suffering of Christ for us. As the verse says, Christmas is a time to thank the Lord for the love that holds us close." Her word reminded me of that passage from Walter Wangerin, Jr.'s remarkable book, _The Book of the Dun Cow,_ where the rooster, Chauntecleer, cries out in the middle of the night to God about the burden of being lonely at the top:

> "I didn't ask for this," he shouted. "You, God—you bound me body and soul to it, and you never told me! Come down out of heaven and tell me why. I can be only one thing around these Hens: a leader, a commander, and ever right and never wrong. Do you suppose that I could put my head down and weep like that boat-headed Dog

you sent me? Of course not! Oh, you know very well.
The Hens would panic and their world collapse. Do you
suppose I could be afraid out loud?...Let the Lord God,"
Chauntecleer roared to the heavens, "let the Lord God
himself come down and stand before me and give an
accounting of himself—that he makes Roosters lonely![3]

Have we ever felt like that?

There's a Bruce Reed of the Grubb Institute in London
who has developed what he calls the Grubb Theory of Oscilla-
tion. This theory says that people tend to oscillate between
two modes of life: extradependence and intradependence. In
the former mode, we are dependent only on ourselves and
our own inner resources for what we're doing and that's okay.
But in the latter mode we need an extra source external to
ourselves—and that's okay too. We may move back and forth
between the two, and it's good to know that both are good
human stances and where we are at the moment. The strong
ones among us, for instance, may at times really have a hidden desire to be held like a little child; which is to say, there
is a need for the strong one to have others minister to him
or her. It's good to recognize that and act on it, else we will
indeed feel loneliness in all its force.

I think of the red-light district here in the Dutch town
that has been my home in recent years, Alkmaar, near
Amsterdam. In Holland prostitution is out in the open
and legal. We have a street that isn't mentioned in the
"one-hour walk" recommended by the local tourist office. From early evening till late at night, women with
very little clothing on sit behind large windows. Between
customers, when the curtains aren't drawn, they watch
television, read, and sometimes knit. One of my children
asked me what the women do when the curtains are
closed. Hiding my confusion and panic, I threw the question back, "Well, what do you think they do?" There was
no panic in Daniel's response. "I think they hug lonely
people."

How true. More than anything else, these ladies are in
the loneliness trade. The forlorn men who wander that
street at night are probably very much in need of being

hugged and listened to. What a pity that hired sex is the only way they can find escape, however briefly, from their particular glass jars.[4]

I'm wondering two things as I read this story. Is Daniel really his son's name or is the son a personification of the perennial Old Testament wisdom figure with his wise response? Second, how much of our own sexual difficulties and abberations are rooted here, in loneliness, in our need to be "hugged" by the bishop, our colleagues, the people? Is anybody aware of our loneliness? (Image problem again.) Do they care? Do we let them know?

That the Lord is my shepherd and I shall not want is true enough, and a deep spiritual relationship with the Lord is a powerful antidote for loneliness; but the Lord still remains in carnational and touches us in other people. He likes to be with us where two or three gather in his name, and he simply loves to be in our company when we break bread with other people. So, before you read any further, lay down this book a minute and call some people now and invite them to dinner.

Now that you've done a good deed (for yourself), let's attend briefly to that adorable and lofty ideal that all priests on the planet should, above all things else, be "pastoral." The idea is neat. The trouble is, however, that the very definition of pastoral is untidy. What exactly _does_ the word imply? We should take this question seriously because we are all under its domination. The best one I know who's had the courage to at least take the word to task in a sensible way is Father George Wilson of Management Design, Inc. of Cincinnati. His ideas are as follows: being pastoral usually suggests in the popular mind (and our own) some emotional down-home, "human" people concerned, not with movements and law and institutions, but with real everyday people in their real everyday crises. We, like Jack Lemmon's Father, Tim Farley, in the movie _Mass Appeal_, try to please everyone, ruffle no one, and slide over making any demands of the people. As Wilson says, in the popular mind:

Being pastoral is being concerned with individuals. Sister does not waste a lot of time on meetings and programs; she is out there caring for Mrs. O'Grady, who is finding it difficult since Charley died, and Mary Jo Jackson, who is pregnant and needs a lot of support because her parents have rejected her. The opposite of a pastoral person is an "administrator" – or, if you really want to hurt someone, a "bureaucrat."

Being pastoral means never saying no. It is unpastoral to tell a family they cannot have their child baptized unless they are willing to give some minimal indication that they believe in something more serious than the Dallas Cowboys. And of course the bishop is very unpastoral if he happens to believe that the local Right-to-Everything crowd is pursuing the wrong strategy for achieving worthy goals he happens to believe in. A pastoral person is an ecclesiastical wimp. The opposite of a pastoral person is someone with principles.

Being pastoral means being totally available. The pastoral person is not allowed to say no to a demand for his or her time or presence. The opposite of being pastoral is having a personal existence – or maybe just putting on the answering service during dinner in the rectory.[5]

I not only agree with his words that sometimes the concept of pastoral can be a rather nasty weapon to rob us of our humanity and principles, but I also agree that equating pastoral with being a warm, clerical fuzzy makes the more introverted, uneffusive thinker feel unworthy and out of it. As Wilson says, "By using the term pastoral to describe a particular kind of personality we could be creating expectations that are very unfair to many dedicated ministers."

And what about the very real issue we've tried to underscore in this book: the building up of a shared and collaborative ministry? Those who do spend themselves tirelessly ministering to individual people in need may in fact be neglecting to build a sense of wider, caring community. We ought to ask ourselves if the community will and can continue to keep on providing such care and services after we've gone.

That's the standard for being truly pastoral. It seems to be the way Jesus went about being pastoral, gathering his twelve, entrusting roles to them and sending them out two by two.

For some priests, intimidated by popular misconceptions, trying to be pastoral means trying to please everyone (a guaranteed formula for failure), and therefore they fail to enunciate any norms. But the point is that if we are so heavily into community, then the community surely has its demands on its members, actual or to be. The feared criticism is that those norms may be oppressive and unbending, and we may lose people in the shuffle. On the other end of the spectrum, our norms may be so loose that we perpetuate a magical and indifferent approach to being a Catholic that is almost tantamount to continued uncommitment. But surely, on behalf of the community, we have a right to raise questions, say, about someone's suitability for marriage or to challenge automatic baptisms of nonpracticing and indifferent Catholics. The pastoral art is not to suppress the issues but to raise them sympathetically with respect for people's individual journeys. I have found it helpful to spell out very carefully in our annual Parish Booklet the expectations of the parish community so that policy is there beforehand as a standard and you don't have to fight each individual case as it comes along.

We must be convinced furthermore that being pastoral *does* involve priorities so that we have to say no to other worthy causes; that our always being totally available morning, noon, and night "may have done more to perpetuate paternalistic and materialistic models of the church than all the other factors combined"; that, like a parent, we have to make certain demands and run the risk of unpopularity; that at times, under the difficulty of a prophetic stance, we may sadly have to ask, "Will you also go away?"; that, finally, being pastoral does not necessarily mean being the world's greatest extrovert, the pied piper of all the kids on the block, the easy conversationalist, or the clerical Leo Buscaglia who specializes in parochial hug therapy. The softer introvert also has gifts that are pastoral as well.

In these days when there are no neat rules we must make more prudential judgments than ever before. Perhaps dioceses ought to inaugurate (as some few have) a pastoral sponsorship or "big brother" program whereby the older, more experienced, and recognized pastors can mentor the younger men. Lord knows we all want to be pastoral and of all the items of praise possible that description would look nicest on our tombstones. It's just that we should have a firmer and clearer and no-nonsense understanding of what it is we're talking about.

I remember at a clergy conference listening to the chancellor explain something about diocesan insurance and the answers he gave to some questions were so ambiguous that I was completely befuddled. Anyway, the whole incident called to mind a hilarious performance (according to the reaction I got) of a Tennessee legislator who had gotten a letter from a constituent demanding to know his view on the "whiskey situation." Here is the lawmaker's reply—something similar to what we've heard many times and (gasp!) perhaps have given once or twice.

> "Dear Friend:
> "I had not intended to discuss the controversial subject at this particular time. However, I want you to know that I do not shun a controversy. On the contrary, I will take a stand on any issue at any time, regardless of how fraught with controversy it may be. You have asked me how I feel about whiskey. Here's how I stand on the question:
> "If, when you say whiskey, you mean the Devil's brew, the poison scourge, the bloody monster that defiles innocence, dethrones reason, destroys the home, creates misery and poverty— yes, literally takes the bread from the mouths of little children; if you mean the drink that topples

*the Christian man and woman from the pinnacle
of righteous, gracious living into the bottomless pit
of degradation, despair, shame and helplessness,
then certainly I am against it with all my power.*

*"But, if, when you say whiskey, you mean the
oil of conversation, the philosophic wine, the ale
that is consumed when good fellows get together,
that puts a song in their hearts and laughter on
their lips and the warm glow of contentment in
their eyes; if you mean Christmas cheer; if you
mean the stimulating drink that puts the spring in
an old gentleman's step on a frosty morning; if
you mean that drink, the sale of which pours into
our treasury untold millions of dollars which are
used to provide tender care for our crippled
children, our blind, our deaf, our dumb, pitiful,
aged and infirm, to build highways, hospitals and
schools, then certainly I am in favor of it.*

*"This is my stand, and I will not com-
promise."*

The pastor was in the hospital. For a while it looked serious. The president of the parish council came to cheer him up. "Father," he said reassuringly, "we don't want you to worry about a thing. Last night at our meeting, we voted 8 to 2 to pray for your recovery."

XII

Partnerships

WE HAVE SPOKEN ABOUT THE REALITY THAT INCREASINGLY WE WILL BE working with several levels of lay and religious co-workers about closer shared and collaborative ministry, about relationships as a key context of our spirituality, and about being pastoral. What is taken for granted in all of this is our capacity to communicate well with and get along well with all of these people. Should we take it for granted that we do? Not really. Because we are typical American males we don't always communicate well. We find it hard to be intimate. Frequently we find it hard to work with some degree of comfort with women, religious or lay, who are more and more becoming our team partners.

Some of this is due to new pressures on us as we have tried to show. It takes a lot of energy to adjust to new identities and roles. But, basically, I think, our problems in

162

communication and intimacy and therefore in working in collaboration stem from the simple fact that we are male. As the *McGill Report on Male Intimacy* put it: we men are "reluctant revealers, cautious confirmers, and emotional evaders." I suppose this stems a great deal from our cultural conditioning and perhaps from some basic biological structure, too. Whatever the reason, it seems that we must be open to those movements today which give us a better way to be masculine and sharing.

I recall reading the article "A New Vision of Masculinity" by Cooper Thompson in *Family Life Educator* (Spring 1986) in which the author was called to a suburban high school to give a guest presentation on male roles. He noticed immediately how four dominant jocks suppressed the expression of any other male trait except what they felt was overtly physical, tough, aggressive, dominant, and even violent. Any different behavior by the other boys in class was scathingly put down by that simple word of ridicule: "fag." He perceived not only a rigid, physical standard being imposed of what it meant to be manly, but, more to the point, what behavior patterns were *not* permitted, namely, anything that smacked of being tender or gentle or, in a word, "feminine." There was no room in these boys for nurture, cooperation, emotional expression, or nonaggressive conflict resolution. So along with the homophobia we described in the chapter on spirituality, there was added misogyny, the fear and hatred of women.

Such twin pressures were seen as operative in a simple test the author always gives and from which he always gets the same response. He asks the kids how they would feel if they woke up tomorrow and discovered they were opposite from the sex they are now. Girls eagerly and consistently speak of the advantage of being a boy: increased independence, career opportunities, decreased risks of physical and sexual assault. The boys, however, express utter disgust and often even refuse to answer the questions. They feel they would have to be weak, cook, be a mother, and "other yukky stuff like that. "

The price paid for these culturally honed images is very high. Boys who grow into tough, competitive men can have little long-term security (all the other aggressive males are climbing the ladder behind them) and experience a greater emotional distance from other people. Studies show that fathers spend very little time interacting with their children, child abusers are predominantly men, and rape may be the fastest growing crime in our country. Is it any wonder that such conditioned boys have trouble as men accepting women as equal, competent partners and find cooperation difficult?

Somewhere in all of this are we priests. Hopefully, not among the child abusers and rapists, of course, but certainly there as powerfully socialized by homophobia and misogyny. We have difficulty expressing our feelings (too feminine), are shy of working with competent women, are threatened by collaboration, and resolve conflicts poorly, usually with a final righteous resort to authority. We indeed are reluctant revealers (few or no intimate close friends), cautious confirmers (how hard to give a compliment!), and emotional evaders (better to walk away). And yet, given all this, we are the ones called in this new church of ours to partnership, to a community of equal disciples, to shared ministries, to basic ecclesial communities. We are the ones who are told that our ministry should be deeply satisfying, generative, and filled with deep relationships. We are the ones that, as a pastoral team, are supposed to model community to the larger parish. No wonder we're resistant, scared, or skeptical.

Nevertheless, we have to face the issue and, in our coming to terms with our partners in ministry, our team, here are suggestions that might be helpful. They are from Sister Fran Ferder and Father John Haegle who themselves work as a team. First of all, there are three reasonable expectations we should have as we approach the arena of partnership and collaboration: (1) that we and they need support for our ministry which means, when you come right down to it, a certain reasonable comfort with one another and a certain predictability of how people will act and react. You can't be walking on eggs all the time with one another; (2) that we and they have opportunities to experience growth in our own creativity and professional lives. We can't lock people in to the extent that they never have the chance to learn and become more – and they certainly shouldn't do that to us. Paid for workshops and seminars should be a part of our contract (and, again, that includes ourselves); and (3) a certain (not perfect) sense of community takes place. There has to be a reasonable bonding in the making.

Second, we ought to pay equal attention to what *not* to expect from any team relationship. There are five items here: (1) we must not be unrealistic and expect no conflict at all. That's not to be this side of the Second Coming. Even the best of families have conflicts; even, for that matter, the first apostolic band; (2) we must not think that we will always be in control in the sense that we will always set the agenda, we will always articulate the vision. We need to tap into and listen to the others; (3) we must not expect to find primary community fulfillment and support from our team. That's too heavy a load to place on them or they on us. They are co-workers, not our lovers; (4) we should not see the team as our family. The parish ministry team is not mom, dad, and the kids; and (5) we must not expect the parish itself to build community if we're not into it in our team.

Finally, in attempting to build some kind of team ministry, there are four guidelines to attend to:

1. All of us must be capable of at least reasonable relationship skills. That means we must have some mechanism for dealing with anger and conflict and how to express our feelings. Since in this area, as we have seen, many of us priests are handicapped by upbringing and culture, it might be wise either to seek any diocesan services that help us to be more comfortable in dealing with our feelings or make a good investment by seeing a clinical psychologist.

2. It is good to program into our relationship shared experiences and celebrations. This means we write into our annual calendar the times we'll be together just to share our feelings. This in no way implies a raw, gut-spilling sensitivity session; rather, it implies a forum to let our thoughts and feelings be known. "You know, at the parish council meeting I was kind of waiting for some kind of backup from you, and I felt disappointed at your silence—and a little hurt to tell the truth." Better to say that than just sit there and stew. Or, as more often for us, we just can't give out anger or conflict signals with grunts, distance, short answers to questions, or just deadly courtesy:

> Well, we've only just got back from Ithaca. Bob is fearfully excited about a new set of burial places, and had evolved an entirely original and revolutionary theory about funerary rites. He's writing a paper that contradicts all of Lambard's conclusions, and I'm helping by toning down his adjectives and putting in depracatory footnotes. I mean, Lambard may be a perverse old idiot, but it's more dignified not to say so in so many words. A bland and deadly courtesy is more devastating; don't you think?[1]

We've got to open our mouths. As for the celebrations, that's time away to relax and laugh. In our parish we build such celebrations in as, for example, a Mystery Bus Ride and an overnight in a cabin at Bear Mountain.

3. Often we do and will get stuck. We want to relate, we want to share, get out our feelings, show our vulnerability—but can't. We just can't. That we have a team at all shows our good will but often we can't get beyond that. This is the time to bring in a facilitator. By word of mouth you'll learn who the good ones are, and it will be well worth the investment to bring that person in to unlock the log jam in a warm and non-threatening way.

4. We should be alert to any levels of pathology among our team members. There may be some psychological illness, some obvious depression that's pulling the whole team down,

and so we have to know whether we are dealing with a well or unwell group, and take some steps to work it out.

I guess, when we come right down to it, in this whole topic of partnerships and shared and collaborative ministries we're basically talking about friendship of some kind or other, and that comes, not from sharing parish information, but from sharing oneself. Not that we need to do this to the same degree with everyone, but there ought to be some level of sharing if our co-workers, our team, our parish is to survive and grow. And when one puts it like this, it's hard to resist being pulled into a reflection on Jesus' own ministry.

He certainly was a good leader and a tough one: he couldn't have endured his passion otherwise. He was outspoken where it was needed and firm in his convictions ("Will you also go away?"). Yet he was also tender for he wept over his friend's death and hugged little kids. He related to women, even the kind one meets at a well. He exposed himself to vulnerability in friendship, else he would not have felt Judas's and Peter's betrayals so much. He gave our mutual love for one another as a compelling sign that we were his disciples. He even gave us a realistic (if hard) pattern for our growth when he implied that the seed with its outer shell around it will never truly live until it lets that shell split open and drop off and thereby lets the kernel be vulnerable to the processes of soil, light, and rain; in short, to death. Only then can it live in another way, in another dimension, into a hundredfold life.

What all this tells us in our context of partnerships is that bonding, friendship, or discipleship—whatever you want to call it—costs. Intimacy and self-disclosure cost. Building a team, a staff, a parish community costs. There's no royal road around it, or, to put it more bluntly scriptural, you can't escape the cross in the pursuit of partnerships.

So, here's our personal challenge as we attempt to come to terms with a church that has decided to go "grassroots," that sees a crying need for community in an ever-increasing, fractured, and divided world, that witnesses our young people hungry for God, desperate for belonging and searching for meaning. There *is* a price to pay for working with and enjoying others. There *is* a cross to be borne for many of us as we move away from the Father of authority to the Father who hugs prodigal children. There *is* a struggle to see our celibacy as a mandate to love more widely rather than more narrowly. There *is* the terrible risk of being rejected if you make yourself vulnerable. There *is* a gamble every time we work with others. But all this, as I'm sure you noticed, is but the paradigm we have from Jesus. And no disciple – not one of us priests – is above his master.

Here's the kind of story that delights us because it vindicates the good sense of the common people. It seems that the monsignor of an inner city parish opened his hall for a meeting of some 200 senior citizens. He opened his remarks by saying, "Ladies and gentlemen, I know that crime is on your mind and I want to tell you that a judge I know was mugged this week. And do you know what he did? He called a press conference and he said to the reporters, "This mugging of me will in no way affect my judgment and decisions in matters of this kind." And an elderly woman stood up in the back of the hall and said, "Then mug him again!"

"Is this St. John's church?" "Yes, and this is Fr. Reiss. May I help you?" "Yes, my name is William Fitzgerald. I'm from the IRS. I'm calling confidentially about a Mr. Ernest Siska of your parish." "Yes?" "Well, Mr. Siska has claimed a tax deduction for a contribution of ten thousand dollars he said he made in cash to your church. In strict confidence, Fr. Reiss, do you remember receiving such a sum from Mr. Siska?" There was a moment's silence. "Well, now, Mr. Fitzgerald, if you will call me tomorrow, just about this time, I assure you the answer to your question will be— yes!"

XIII

If I Were King

WE'RE AT THAT POINT WHEN WE CAN SLIP INTO FANTASY A BIT AS WE exclaim, "Oh, if only I were king for a day!" Or, in our case, bishop. What would we priests do? What changes would we make? If we were invited to the bishop's annual national conference in Washington to give them a major address and we had their undivided attention, what would we say in reference to ourselves? As we ponder our answer, we must not automatically assume that all bishops are indifferent or in-

169

sensitive. In fact, all thoughout this book I have tried to quote
from as many of them as I practically could, those who seem
forward looking and have something to say. So, assuming we
had our chance to plead our case and some receptive men
(hopefully including our own bishop), what *would* we say?
I can't speak for you, but I'll plunge in and uphold the tradition by making seven suggestions to our bishops:

1. *Support and appreciate the pastor's redefined role.* Bishops,
you have to remember that you're dealing with your ir-
replaceable front line men, those who are your extensions and
translators. You have to remember also that we are not only
going through dramatic changes but that we are also expected
to be the agents of change for the lay people. So, you may
have to redefine your concept of what makes a "good" pastor.
A good pastor is not only one who dispenses the sacraments –
as important as that is – but also one who builds community.
The pastor is not primarily a sacrament giver, nor a brick and
mortar man, but one who really gathers the people and gives
meaning to their lives and invites them into the larger story
of God's love in Christ. I guess I'm saying that what you think
makes a "good" priest is the way you will react, recognize,
reward, and promote vocations.

2. *Affirm and listen to your priests.* Many bishops are realizing
that priests are becoming a rare breed and fall above the
overall national death rate for men in their age categories –
due, likely, to burn-out from overwork from their decreasing
numbers. Many of you, therefore, are striving for programs
to affirm and relax your priests, programs like Emmaus and
the like. But there has to be more than that. There has to be
personal recognition by phone, letter, or visit. I know from
talking to other priests from around the country and in my
own diocese that this does not often happen. As Father
Vincent Dwyer says in his Genesis II program, priests are
called to be leaders and to affirm others in their uniqueness

and beauty. Yet they can't do this unless they are affirmed and know that they are special. "But most priests," he says, "don't believe that they are special. Most priests feel very insecure, very threatened...and they ache." Dwyer reports that when he speaks to the Sierra clubs he always gets asked, "What do you do about the lack of vocations?" He turns the question around and asks them, "Why don't you pay attention to the vocations you already have? How many of you affirm your priests, tell them how much you need them, tell them of their beauty and their worth, how important they are to your life?" He is asking this of laypeople. How much more can we ask this of you, our bishops? And why shouldn't you ask this of us?

Okay. How about three nosegays (remember that word?) from Peters and Waterman's *In Search of Excellence*—what they say about the worldly kingdom's road to success:

"You know, one of the things that strikes me most about McDonalds is their people orientation. During the seven years I was at McKinsey, I never saw a client that seemed to care so much about its people"(p. xvii).

"There is one critical cultural difference, however, that does seem to foster productivity through people in Japan...treating people—not money, machines, or minds—as the natural resource may be the key to it all"(p. 39).

"People tune out if they feel they are failing, because the 'system' is to blame. They tune in when the system leads them to believe they are successful"(p. 58).

3. *Reeducate and retrain us toward collaboration.* Our lifestyles tend to be that of lone rangers. We are taught to perform: Mass, sacraments, blessing, etc. We are not taught to enable ministry or witness in the world. One thing that worries me about all of this lay ministry explosion of courses and degrees is that they are simply raising the frustration quotient of those same laypeople when they run into the clergy roadblock. It's

not that we don't want to have their collaboration, it's that we're not used to it, we're afraid of it. We need retraining— and retraining in many instances *with* the laypeople. These are increasingly our co-workers.

In the February 21, 1985 issue of *Origins* there is an account of the Anglican "Lay Academy" of California which gives us a good model. The curriculum involves clergy and laity. As Jean Haldane, speaking to the consultation group on adult ministries at the Cardinal Spellman retreat center in New York says, "The content of the courses and the style of learning were directed toward roles, church, and world congregation. . . . The main thrust of the Academy is to help the laity find their ministry in the world and their sense of prayer and mission. The methodology is aimed at uncovering what adults had already learned from life, formal education and the church enabling them to reexamine, relearn, integrate, let go and then move on. The clergy in this program see that, when they gave lay people to each other, the church came alive. As one of them put it, "We've rediscovered baptismal ministry." Haldane comments, "The clergy—after a moment of panic at the possibility of the laity taking over—found their jobs enlarged in support of personal transitions and requests for further education. . . . The associate rector summed it up this way, "This vestry now spends as much time talking about faith and spiritual development, and support of the ministry of the laity, as about getting the roof repaired and the parking lot paved.' "

So, to the bishops we say: we need your help in making a transition of viewpoint, of priority, of learning how to listen, to move, and enable groups to work together with the laity in our common enterprise. We need some reeducation.

And yet, I want to make this point strongly: this reeducation is not just to learn collaboration, but to truly become very professional ourselves with a strong sense of our identity, competence, and abilities. There is, I think, an insight that we might ponder from Thomas Archdeacon's review of Jay

Dolan's book *The American Catholic Experience.* After a generally favorable review, he writes:

A social history of Catholicism, ironically, will also have to be more concerned about the present and even the future in order to see the past in perspective. It will have to deal at greater length than Mr. Dolan does with those who have walked or drifted away from the church during the pontificates of Paul VI and John Paul II. Perhaps most of all, it will have to deal with the growing body of educated and able Catholics who want access to the sacraments of the church but who feel little need for it otherwise. Many among those "communal Catholics," as the Rev. Andrew M. Greeley has termed them in another context, are bemused by the 'amateurization' in the church. It has left its clergy wanting to dispense social services that their congregations can obtain for themselves and has shifted religious duties to the laity, including the theological education of the young, for which the pastors seem to feel less professional responsibility than in the past. What relationships communal Catholics decide to maintain with the church, or to forego, will be a critical development for the social history of American Catholicism in the late 20th century.[1]

The author here hits on some notions that have to be seriously considered, namely, the evangelization of the communal Catholic. But he also challenges us to more professionalism. Perhaps implicit in his words is that no amount of degreed laity ought to preempt the professionalism of the clergy — and we need help to find a balance here and even to address the issue properly.

4. *Promote a better image (and vocations).* We've seen that often, for the various reasons we have explored, the public image of the priesthood is poor both for outsiders and frequently for the priest himself. We need a good PR program. You bishops should cut out a sizable amount of the national budget for promoting our image. Perhaps here is where you ought to most imitate the children of the darkness in their

savvy. We need recruiting ads like the Marines, or such, that give the message that we are something, that we count, make a difference.

"Caring runs in the veins of the managers of these institutions. People are why those managers are there, and they know it and live it. The orientation is bone-deep and embedded in the language itself"(Peters and Waterman, p. 239).

5. *Create a sense of purpose, a sense of being a part of a larger enterprise.* Yes, I know that you say our faith should be enough and we should silently struggle in the Lord; but we are human and need a sense of being part of a larger purpose. We need to know what's going on; chancery communication is poor. Few avenues exist to make our feelings and thoughts known. There is a sense of things always being decided on top. We have to feel that we're on a winning team and are engaged in an overall purpose if we are to go out there and work for and with the people.

"The top performers create a broad, uplifting, shared culture, a coherent framework....Nothing is worse for morale than a lack of information down in the ranks. I call it NETMA—Nobody Ever Tells Me Anything—and I have tried to minimize the problem" (p. 51, p. 267).

6. *Gingerly I suggest we need better bishops.* You keep sending those three names into Rome as potential other bishops. The trouble is that these are men you work with all the time, whose training tends to be narrow and confined to chancery goings on. It's understandable you would choose someone like yourself (clone yourself as some whisper), someone you feel you can trust and not be off the wall. But by consistently choosing office men, you keep overlooking the trench men, the prophets in the street. I suggested in the body of the book that a law ought to be passed that no one can be considered as bishop material until he has spent at least ten years in the trenches. We need men from there. The view is simply different there: the vision, the attitude, the practical theology,

the experience of community. Please, at least one of those three names should be "from the ranks." As Juan Segundo notes, Rome's present practice in choosing bishops for their loyalty to the Vatican rather than for their leadership may mean that "the new episcopate will lose a large part of its present ability to contain and direct the popular church." In short, Vatican appointments, fed in by you, may have a greater impact than its statements – and we respectfully ask you to remember that.

I suppose it would not be amiss here to tell you, bishops, that at the 1983 convention of the National Association of Church Personnel Administrators, the moderator of the session about the spirituality of the diocesan priest wrote on the blackboard the most common image of the bishop as the average priest saw him. When the tally was in, the top prevailing image was "boss" – not friend, co-worker or fellow priest. I suppose we should not make too much of this because, in a sense, something like that would be expected in any superior-subordinate equation. Still, as I said, men always drawn off the "top" and not from the ranks, bring such biased imagery with them. At least you should be concerned and, I would hope, nervous until you could move the boss image somewhat closer to friend or brother image. "No longer do I call you servants, for the servant does not know what his master is doing; but I have called you friends. . . ." (John 15:14)

"Burns speaks most convincingly of the leader's need to enable his followers to transcend daily affairs. He begins by faulting earlier students of leadership for their preoccupation with power, suggesting that such attention blinded them to the far more important task of instilling purpose"(p. 83).

"Marriott, Ray Kroc, Bill Hewlett, and Dave Packard, Levi Strauss, James Cash Penney, Robert Wood Johnson. . .*believed* in the customer. They *believed* in granting autonomy, room to perform. They *believed* in open doors, in quality"(p. 319).

7. *Read two books if no others.* The first book every bishop

should read is John L. Mckenzie's *Authority in the Church*. It gives a good historical approach to authority's origins and use in the church and is an excellent context for its exercise. The second book is Peter and Waterman's *In Search of Excellence*. You simply cannot read this secular book without ecclesiastical applications forcing themselves on you at every page. In fact, what comes through so often is an almost religious underpinning, transcendental talk, and basic gospel principles. Any and all priests reading this book should rush right out and purchase and send these books to their bishops forthwith.

That's my seven suggestions. I'm sure the readers of this book have their own to add and perhaps far more perceptive ones. So, at this point we're ready to sign off this chapter. Usually, as you know, it's with a story. This time, however, I want to close with some quotations that I would hope you would meditate on and find full of promise. They are chosen because, I feel, they put in perspective so much of our doomsdaying. Dare I tell you that there are seven of them?

1. "The Church is that community which results from the outer communication of Christ's message and the inner gift of God's love" – (Bernard Lonergan).

2. "Madison Jones stopped by here a few Saturdays ago and sat a good while. . . . It seems that his wife and four children are Catholics. He said he guessed he was intellectually convinced but just didn't have the faith. My cousin's husband who also teaches at Auburn came into the Church last week. He had been going to Mass with them but never showed any interest. We asked how he got interested and his answer was that the sermons were so horrible, he knew there must be something else there to make the people come"(Flannery O'Connor, *The Habit of Being*, p. 348).

3. "[The pre–Vatican II church] was imperfect; it was culture-bound; but it was a church of prayer and alive with

movements. The American liturgical movement was more than fifty years old at the time of the council; the literary revival, thirty years or more. The movement to recover the original charisms of the religious orders and to adapt them to the modern world had been launched by Pius XII in the early 1950s. The social action movements which united the best of the clergy and the laity in the Depression years had grown and multiplied—among them, the Catholic Worker movement, the interracial movement, the various Catholic Labor movements, the Christian Family movements, etc., etc., —all had plowed the ground. When Pope John convoked the council he could say that the church was ready (Abigail McCarthy in *Commonweal*, Nov. 15, 1985, p. 634).

4. "History's lessons are not all negative and foreboding. One of the most positive, optimistic, and uplifting has been the appearance of prophetic figures whose voices have been raised to center the gaze of the people of God on high spiritual ideals and thus proved strong counterforces to negative and corroding influences.... The history of the Universal Church is replete with men and women of this character....

"Nor has the church in the United States been lacking these prophetic voices.... One thinks, for example, of the following among the myriad men and women whose writings, actions, and lives of model Christian endeavor have lighted the way for thousands of their co-religionists in the United States to whom they bequeathed movements and organizations that still endure and contribute notably to the present generation of American Catholics. One has only to name them to know what is meant: Elizabeth Seton (Catholic schools), Katherine Drexel (the apostolate to the Blacks), Virgil Michel (liturgical reform), John A. Ryan (social action), Cesar Chavez (unionization of oppressed laborers), ... and there are scores of others who in their quiet and self-effacing way have lived the faith in love in a manner that has given courage and hope to their contemporaries and to those who have come after them. Here, then, has been a lesson of history from the

American past that merits the serious consideration of all who call themselves Catholic" (John Tracy Ellis, *The Critic,* Winter, 1985, p. 38-39).

5. "People remain [in the church] because they know there is something more important than any of these things [ordaining married men or women]. What? People remain Catholic because they believe Jesus is present in the Church, despite everything. God's life is shared with people through the sacraments despite the people who administer and receive them. We believe that God who created the universe is humble enough to be present to us in pieces of bread we can hold in our hands" – (John Garvey).

6. "My thesis is simple. There are quiet qualities of leadership that burn like fire in the soul. One does not need to be flamboyant, charismatic, or even outgoing to provide effective leadership. Quiet qualities are God-given and form the basis for one's responses in leadership situations. They become the convictions that launch action and direct a leader from within. . . .

"I have talked with hundreds of pastors who struggle with their style of ministry. My counsel is always the same: do not copy anyone else and do not succumb to peer pressure. Be God's man! Be yourself! But do be an umbrella man. Be sure that you are fulfilling your calling to be a servant to the church. Make sure your ministry provides for and makes room for the ministry of others" (Pastor William Yaeger, First Baptist Church, *Who's Holding the Umbrella?* p. 19, 30).

7. "When I was much older, I returned to the Church. I did so very gingerly, first peering in for a moment, letting my eyes adjust to the lights and shadows of the place. I knew that it had changed, but I had no feeling for what it had become.

"Gradually, I saw that it was a sweeter and softer place than it had been. The anger had gone out of it, that dark punitive vibration, the Pauline scowl. The Church was more habitable now, more human. Perhaps it was also that the anger had departed from me as well.

"The old black mystery was gone, too. I regretted that, for a while. I missed the Latin, the elaborate, enameled ritual, the high rhetoric and hieratic pageantry. The sixties seemed to have left their mark of fatuity upon the institution. The Mass that I remembered from my youth ended with the magnificent *Ita, missa est.* Now I heard a priest one Sunday morning finish off his performance by saying, "The Mass is ended. Have a nice day." I saw another priest, a TV priest, saying Mass in vestments adorned with a happy sunburst design and the words, 'Here comes the Son.' I wished then to sign up for the heresy of the retrograde, those Catholics who had begun staging Latin Masses in defiance of Rome.

"But I came to see that perhaps the change was just as well. The departure of the densely brocaded mysteries, it may be, allowed one to confront more simply the real mysteries of things.

"I came to see that the Church was not the Father turned into an architecture of eternity, not an inflexible outward form, but was a medium through which the soul might aspire. I saw that struggling toward God was a process, an active and not a passive enterprise.

"I went back to the Church in part for the sake of my son Jamie. In any case, I no longer sought authority there, the comfort of its domination, the principle of the father. The Church now seemed a smaller thing, more on equal terms with the world. The Church has grown a little confused, like everyone, I thought. The confusion diminished the Church, but was in some ways endearing" – (Lance Morrow, *The Chief*).

The Doctor went to see him, but the Pastor didn't go.
For the Doctor had been sent for, but the Pastor didn't know.
The Doctor got rewarded with a handsome little check.
But the Pastor for not knowing simply got it in the neck.

XIV

Novus Habitus Mentis

As WE APPROACH THE CONCLUSION OF THIS BOOK, I'll TURN MORE pedantic and move away from our personal concerns, which are surely legitimate, to the larger vision underlying this book. This vision permeates the various discussions and recommendations and at times appears briefly in explicit form. I want to share more openly where I think we're going and why I took the approach that I did. In my heart I realize some will disagree, but I have to hope that even disagreement will facilitate both our own search in difficult times and that of the church we love and serve so dearly.

My vision is summed up in the Latin title of this chapter:

"A new habit of the mind," or more colloquially, a new way of seeing, a new way of being church, a new attitude. The phrase belongs to Pope Paul VI and I have found its truth most forcefully expressed in two recent dramatic forms, one closely related to the other. The first is the revised *Code of Canon Law* promulgated by Pope John Paul II on January 25, 1983, and the other is an unusual meeting held in Bruges in June 1985."[1]

The revised Code has a Bill of Rights, and among these are two principles, reflecting the decrees and spirit of Vatican II *(Lumen Gentium, 37)*: consultation and collegiality. The Code gives a great deal of moral weight to both. In fact, consultation is listed as one of the fundamental freedoms, rights, and legal qualifications in the Catholic church, and that accounts for our chapter on authority and leadership. We might want to get out our tome of Canon Law and look, for example, at canon 212:2 where it says, "The Christian faithful are free to make known their needs, especially their spiritual ones, and their desires to the pastors of the church." Paragraph 3 of the same code states:

> In accord with the knowledge, competence and pre-emenience which they possess, they have the right and even at times a duty to manifest to the sacred pastors their opinion on matters which pertain to the good of the Church, and they have a right to make their opinion known to the other Christian faithful, with due regard for the integrity of faith and morals and reverence toward their pastors, and with consideration for the common good and the dignity of persons.

We should note, by the way, that in canon law "pastor" also includes the pope and the bishop as well as the parish priest.

To round out the picture, canon 228:2 says that lay persons of competence are qualified as experts and advisors both individually and in councils. Consultative bodies as a church-polity fact are found in canons 460 to 468, finance committees in canons 492, 493, and 1277; presbyteral councils in canons 495 to 502; pastoral councils in canons 511 to 514 and local councils in canons 536 and 537. I suppose the fundamental canon concerning consultation in the church is canon 127 which says that if the superior (read: pope, bishop, priest) is obliged to consult and does not, then his action is invalid; that no superior is to act contrary to advice offered him if that advice is unanimous or arrived at by consensus unless there is an overriding reason to do so. Interestingly enough, this is not a new thought for it was in the old Code of 1917! Anyway, both the letter and, above all, the spirit of the revised Code call for genuine and wide consultation and that principle is what you have read both in and in between the lines of this book as we searched for new ways of pastoring.

As for collegiality, there are three meanings to this word in a church context. Strictly speaking, the theological meaning is that derived from Scripture and refers to Peter and the Eleven as a college and then by extension to the pope and his bishops and to the the bishops and his presbyters. Here we have a kind of sacramental sign of unity. The second meaning is strictly legal, derived from old Roman law; it implies a group of equals who transfer their powers to a board of directors or to an individual. This is a democratic process in action, decisions of which derive from majority rule. Finally, there is our own peculair American concept derived from our American culture from education, politics, school boards, business, and the Protestant denominations. Our notion of collegiality means participation. No wonder there is tension! When Rome hears us use "collegiality," it feels we want to determine everything in the church by majority vote, while normally we mean only that we want greater participation.

In any case, these notions indicate that there are two forms of governance in the church: the consultative form *demanded* of diocesan and parish church leaders and the collegial form required for voluntary associations. The reason that we have the two forms is that, unlike the Protestant denominations, we are an episcopal not a congregational church. We run by decision derived from consensus and consultation and they run by majority vote. This is why I opted for Rabbi Friedman's style of leadership: one that listened sincerely and carefully but then reached decision in solitude.

We should not miss, however, the point the code is making. Although, strictly speaking, the church is and will likely remain legally episcopal in structure, the revised *Code of Canon Law* comes down heavily on the side of the *moral* force of consultation, consensus, and collegiality as a lifestyle. Again, this is why we spoke of shared and collaborative ministry. Once more, what has changed, you see, is not the legal formulations but rather the very way of being church, the way of seeing, the "new habit of the mind" through which law is interpreted. To further underscore this "new habit of the mind," you might want to turn to the very brief introduction of Pope John Paul II to the revised Code. He went to great lengths to point out that basically the consultative and collegial attitudes in the Code are a direct outcome of the spirit of Vatican II. In fact, he lists six basic conciliar principles which were incorporated into the Code.

1. The "genuine image" of the church is the People of God.

2. Authority is seen in terms of service rather than power.

3. Communion is important and is realized between the universal and local churches.

4. All the members of the church, not just the clergy, participate in the threefold priestly, prophetic, and kingly office of Christ.

5. There is a Bill of Rights for all members, especially the laity.

6. The church is committed to ecumenism.

The reason I bring this up and walk with you through all of these canonical pathways is to point out once again that the approach of this book is not merely personal but finds its core in the documents of Vatican II and the derivative revised Code. We may argue about the practical translations I have given but not about the basic change of focus which says that all the people are the church and that we leaders have to move from former positions of managers who provide services for spiritual consumers and clients to being animators of active participants.

The other form that, to my mind, summed up the "new habit of the mind" is less known but no less global than the Code. In June 1985, Christiane Brusslmans gathered a symposium on the local church at Bruges in Belgium. The five continents were represented. The point of the symposium was to see what was happening in the local churches throughout the world. Four models emerged.

The first model might be called the Liberation Model of local church. Most of us are familiar with this model from the media. (We might be more familiar with the Vatican's negative view of liberation theology, although a new, more favorable, report was released in April 1986.) This model flourishes in the Third and Fourth Worlds where cultural and economic oppression and persecution are present. Here there is a priest with some sisters and a lay staff. They cover what is called a "pastoral zone," at whose center the many various parish communities or base communities meet several times a year. Meanwhile, during the rest of the time the lay-led base communities meet to sing and to tell their stories and then counterpoint them against the biblical story of redemption and see where they intersect in their lives. They develop ministries, such as the ministry of storytelling, poetry, prayer leading, comforter, freedom fighter (the one who has enough moxie to talk to the mayor), and missionary.

No one is passive in these base communities and, when they meet to study and pray the issues of the gospel, they expect some action to ensue. In a steady line they move to issues of community, to works of mercy, to advocacy, to system change. This model, as you realize, differs radically from the high individualism of our American church—an individualism which Robert Bellah and his associates point out in their book *The Habit of Being* is enshrined in the very language we use. As Father Bertran Griffin[1] puts it, they go from Bible study to community to social change; we go from Bible study to therapy! In this model an involved laity is the key, laity who are not helping out the church in the pinch of priest shortage, but who see themselves in a new way: as the church.

The second model is the Four Seasons or Renew Model. This is the European model and the quickest and most accurate thing that can be said is that the Catholic church is dead in Europe. Church going is extremely rare—about 3 percent, for example, for the church's eldest daughter. Rectories all over Europe have been taken over by the Yuppies who turn them into grand houses or condos. A pastor, almost always old and/or sick, may have as many as forty-five parishes to take care of. People come to him at the "four seasons" of their lives: birth, first communion, marriage, and death—in two out of four of these occasions they're carried there! But from the ashes of the collapse of the church and the priesthood the people who are left are learning to be church in a new way. To these scattered remnants, the priest is the "animator" or facilitator. The laity is being renewed as church in small base communities.

The third model is the Catechetical or Hospitality Model of Africa. Here the church is new again (used to flourish there in the first four centuries but collapsed not only from Moslem inroads but from its unwillingness to adapt to the local culture). Being new, everyone has within recent years gone through the long-term catechemenate (transported to us as the RCIA). There is a small number of clergy here also who work in a vast pastoral zone in which the small base communities gather for the eucharist or from which the eucharist is brought to them. This is a vibrant, growing church of connected communities into which no one may be baptized unless he or she promises to undertake a ministry.

The fourth model of local church is the Diaspora Model of the Asian and Eastern blocs. Here the church is a minority and, to a small or large degree, oppressed. To be church here is to have a firm understanding of oneself and one's commitment. This is the witness stance, being present in a hostile culture.

There is no fifth model of local church because the last continent, North America, could offer no model. We haven't worked it through yet. Some of us are still tied to the old 1917 Code model of a parish as a specified territory, basically a political unit, which was set up for two simple and direct purposes: (1) to provide pastoral service for the people of the territory, and (2) to provide revenue for the pastor.

But in the revised Code of 1983 the parish model is that of community and pastoral care – whether the pastor is in residence or not. The community's integrity is maintained. Again, in the revised Code the parish is not a territory but a community, and therefore when, in the light of the priest shortage, we start to talk about consolidation we have to be careful that we mean consolidating parish *services,* not *communities.* The communities must stay intact. This, of course, brings us right back to what we have been saying in this book: we have to see the church and ourselves in a new way and with new attitudes. Moreover, we have to approach our task no longer as managers but as animators and see our parishes no longer as plants but as communities.

You might want to take these models of the global local church and compare them with Father Philip Murnion's American models.[2] He points out the surveys which compare us to Western Europe and find that God and religion are far more important to us. The only trouble is, he reminds us, is that such high degree of profound faith has little impact on our lives, families, and work. In short, though professedly religious we are basically secular: not losing our faith nor hating it but merely isolating it to a private zone. We have lost the link between faith and life and so our American task is to relink them, to reconstruct a Catholic spirituality that does.

To do this, we must once more look to community, for the sociological truism is that living according to one's faith depends a great deal on the support of a community, the affirmations, rewards, signals, and values that "significant others" give off. Faith-and-life linkage, then, depends on community but that, as we all know, has suffered deterioration in the extreme. Not only do we have high mobility, an enshrined, almost pathological individualism, but the very unit, the family, is splintered by divorce – the world's highest rate. This is reflected in the low participation rate at Sunday Mass: about one-third of the Catholics attend; and many, when they do, have no community loyalty but, like trained consumers, pick out the parish that pleases them as well as the rules for personal and social behavior. They look upon their relationship to the universal and local church not as communal, committed, and active but as private, voluntary, and passive.

So, what do we do? We do what we have been describing in this book: We plan a strategy, one way or another, to build parish community. Father Murnion gives us five models or approaches to building community:[2]

The first is the traditionalist approach, gathering people around the Baltimore catechism and general Tridentine nostalgia, the usual canonized ideal period where priests were priests (read: in the rectory) and women were women (read: in the home).

The second is the sectarian or remnant approach. Gather the folks into a small band of the elect whether of the prophetic, heroic kind (e.g. the *Catholic Worker* people) or the praise kind (charismatics) and therefore be counterculture. Leave the masses, the half hearted and half-committed, to themselves.

The third model or approach to community is the intimacy model of personal relationships (e.g. marriage-encounter style) and other ways that groups can break through the feelings of alienation.

The fourth approach is to settle for a parish that is a productive association of groups who find in the parish a variety of pleasing and fulfilling activities but without trying to bind the various groups together. The emphasis here is on service, providing something for everybody within a general religious context.

The fifth is the solidarity model which moves beyond the circle or circles of intimacy toward the stranger and others who are not our own. The solidarity here is with the whole Catholic tradition, linking present to past and belief to action. There is a common mission, and the Sunday liturgy, well done, is the kind that attracts, binds, and challenges. There are strong symbols of identity and sound structures.

All of these models or approaches have good points but the last one is obviously more balanced. But again, as in the international models of local church, all these national models are geared toward community and, except for the first one, have various commitments to the people seeing themselves as church and consequently the priests seeing themselves in a new service and enabling role.

In a word, the local church, both here and abroad, our arena of ministry, is by any standard becoming more participatory and that's a fact we have to come to terms with. We are in the painful seismic shift of seeing our parishes, traditionally (in our experience) consumer- and client-oriented, moving toward congregations that are involved in shared and collaborative ministry, congregations which are moving from the masses who receive our ministrations to a people being church in a new way. Our people are metamorphosing from mere-helpers-by-permission to emerging ministers-by-baptismal-right. The pastor is being challenged to change from a service provider to an animator, from dominating to consulting. Pastors are beginning to realize that they need fewer parish council members (although important) and more organizers of community.

This point of view received some strong support from an unusually self-critical report issued by the Vatican in May 1986 entitled, "Sects or New Religious Movements: Pastoral Challenge." It acknowledged that the various sects or cults were flourishing, in part because "needs and aspirations which are seemingly not being met in the mainline churches." The report called for creating "more fraternal" church structures, ones "more adapted to people's life situations" and that "preaching, worship and community prayer should not necessarily be confined to traditional places or worship." And all this implies (bishops and pastors, please note) that we should be sensitive about the size of parishes for the chances of community and "more fraternal structures" appear to decrease in direct ratio to size.

And all this, you see—all these megatrends (to refer to our first chapter)—is what is behind this book. We indeed may be in a confusing period of transition but the church is far from defunct, and parish life, convoluting from service station to community, is here to stay. And in this role of change, this "new habit of the mind," we are chosen to lead. The spirit of Vatican II, the revised Code of church law, the exchange of models of local church—all are pointing, not to demise, but to rebirth. And in this rebirth we are chosen to be midwives. The gathering of peoples around the word, the intersecting of their story with God's story, the emerging ministries are all signs of new life. And in this new life we are chosen to be animators. How scary, how challenging, how exciting—yet how familiar: "And they devoted themselves to the apostles, teaching and fellowship, to the breaking of the bread and the prayers."

The mother came into her son's bedroom and said, "Come on, get up. It's Sunday. You'll be late for church."

"I don't want to go to church!

"Don't be silly. You've got to go to church."

"No, I don't. I don't want to go for two reasons. First, they don't like me and second, I don't like them."

"Nonsense. You have to go and I'll give you two reasons why. First, you're fifty-one years old and second, you're the pastor!"

The pastor went into the pulpit one Sunday morn-
ing before Mass and announced that he had been
transferred to another parish. He continued, "The
same Jesus who led me to this parish is now
leading me to another." Whereupon the congrega-
tion stood and began the opening hymn, "What a
Friend We Have in Jesus...."

XV

Take Heart, Father!

THIS FINAL SHORT CHAPTER IS BY WAY OF AN EPILOG. IN FACT, IT WILL
look suspiciously like an extended homily. I suppose that's
inevitable because it is not only a reflection on the previous
pages but a tribute to my peers.

Looking back over these pages, I feel that I did not do
justice to the real pain that I have seen and heard from priests
who truly sense that they are far less needed than in previous
times. In one of those movements of history in the modern
age, the church in the eighteenth century turned to the hierarchy to help it hold the traditional line in the aftermath of the
French Revolution and its excesses and the onslaught of its
brand of democracy. Then it turned to the professionals (the
religious orders) when it decided in the nineteenth century
to come to (limited) terms with democracy and set up com-

191

peting health and welfare systems (schools, hospitals, etc.). Now, in the twentieth century, we're in a different turn of events and to combat the sterility and nihilism of a failed liberalism, the church has turned to those, as ones born out of due time, who are simply the people, and especially and preferentially the poor. In a word, the church in this day and age has turned not only to the Christian community as the locus of preserving and evangelizing the gospel, but to small communities, base communities, if you will, and to the charisms of the people who make them up.

In this analysis, we can see how our priestly role has changed. In the first two movements (valuable and needed at the times I would submit), we were in a privileged part of pyramid structure with sharply defined roles and status. We led, we taught, we gave the sacraments, we were in the relationship of the adult parent to little children vis-à-vis our people. But in this current movement—this movement of small communities of mutually shared charisms—our pyramid has collapsed and we find ourselves sitting in a circle. We're like the man who fell from the sky. We're bewildered and dazed. We're not sure where we fit in. We suddenly realize that we haven't the skills required for dialogue and collaboration—and maybe we don't even have the heart for it. We find ourselves more in the relationship of a parent to his or her adult children with minds and lifestyles of their own. We've not adjusted yet to this new situation. The pain is real. It's deep. It's everywhere among the clergy. It's not only "Who am I?" but "Why am I?" that bugs them.

No wonder priests hesitate to become pastors and take on administration—much like the sisters who are less and less willing to take on the jobs of principals and superiors: they are not trained in the new leadership styles. It seems that what we priests really want as an ideal is a small parish with no school, no associate and, in our more depressed moments, no people! I guess in the old days we were quite ready for the tried and true asceticisms of prayer, fasting, celibacy, and service. This new asceticism is something else again: the asceticism of staff meetings, parish council meetings, and committee meetings. It makes one long for the tamer flagellations of yesteryear.

Well, we've tried to take note of this pain several times and in various ways throughout the book, and I repeat the theme here, just to let my brothers know that I am sensitive to it and wanted, once more, to give it some space.

But there's another theme that I want to emphasize before we leave these pages. I spoke of our new role in the shared and collaborative ministry of local community as enabling and freeing the charisms of the people. I want to state here as loudly as I can that this kind of facilitating and promoting, once you get on to it, is positively joyous. I don't think I made that point strongly enough. Our leadership, our orchestrating the people into a holy harmony (a favorite metaphor of mine), is truly exciting and fulfilling. There is not only a glorious liberty in not having to play God, but there is positive fellowship and excitement in being a part of the community; of standing there, so to speak, like a clerical Leonard Bernstein, lifting the baton and drawing notes and instruments into marvelous sounds that break the silences of isolation, despair, and loneliness. There is a joy in not being the whole orchestra and a greater joy in leading the many gifts into a single harmony. This is a leadership that is fulfilling, that allows your weakness to be known and shown, but that gives you a privileged place, instinctively honored by a special sacrament beyond baptism, within that community called the people of God.

I want to transmit some of that excitement, if I can, because twenty of my thirty-one years as a priest have been spent that way; that is, spent in finding my role within the community (not above it) and in that place, discovering a firm and unambiguous identity as leader. Again, to return to my favorite metaphor, I assume that Mr. Bernstein does not fancy himself better than the flute player or above him or her, but he must know, and the flute player must know, that when he picks up that baton, there is something different happening than when they eat at McDonald's together or socialize. There is a charism of leadership, of orchestration, that calls forth the charism of flute playing and violin playing and oboe playing into a synergy of something new, something more than the sum total of the instruments and players. And that, as the kids say, is neat.

Or, if you want to be a speck more analytical, some theologians are saying that if it is true (and it seems to be so) that reform and renewal are coming not from the top but from the bottom, from small Christian communities, then they have tracked this development into a five-stage movement: (1) There is the church of traditional activities and devotions which are geared to personal piety; (2) then comes the church of small communities with shared ministries and common liturgy and prayer; (3) then this type of church begins to address and serve society; (4) then it accepts a prophetic role in society; and, finally, (5) it organizes into prophetic action and transformations of society – a real participatory, local church rooted in the culture and experiences of its people. Even if a portion of this scenario is valid, we can see how critical we are to this whole developing enterprise. We can see the powerful role of leadership obviously very much needed; that is to say, our premiere role through ordination. That is to say, our challenge and promise.

I tell you this: it will be and is harder. It was much easier in the old days to bark out orders on Sunday and go to bed on Monday till the next weekend. This current and future style of leadership, this attention to this parish community's charisms, requires much more listening and mutual respect, much more interaction and much more time. But, you know, it's like the old saying: better to have loved and lost than never to have loved at all. In the old way, it was safer to seclude oneself in clericalism, secure in the possession of all the charisms and sole dispenser of the channels of grace. In this new way, in this "family" setting, it's messier. It even means being ministered to as well as ministering – and, believe me, that is hard. But the compensations! – they make it all worth while. What are they? They are the ways we are humanized without losing our leadership and the ways we find the two things we most need these days: laughter and forgiveness.

Brothers, we are the visionary coordinators of today. We have always been, especially in this country, very close to our people—which is why we have no tradition of anticlericalism. In this sense, we have anticipated the current movement of the Spirit in turning to the gifts of ordinary people to offset the materialism and emptiness of a world ever threatened by extinction whether quickly from the bomb or slowly from befouling and poisoning our environment. At this critical point in our history, it is we who are called upon to lead and inspire. And we can do it. And we will.

Take heart, Father.

Well, as is our custom, we end with a story but, perhaps, not quite a story. Rather, a parable, one I think, especially suited for God's post-conciliar priests, one that tells of rerouted dreams and glory in unexpected places. It goes like this:

Once upon a time in a forest, three young trees were growing side by side. As they grew, they shared with one another their dreams of what they would become when they grew to be big trees. The first tree said, "My dream is to become part of a luxurious home where many famous people come and go and admire the grain and color of my wood."

The second tree said, "My dream is to become the tall mast of an elegant sailing vessel that journeys to the seven seas."

And the third said, "My dream is to become part of a great tower, so high that it will inspire people who look at it. People will come from all over the world to see it."

*And so the young trees dreamed. Eventually
the trees grew to maturity and were cut
down. The first didn't become a part of a luxurious home, as it had dreamed, but instead
some of its wood was fashioned into a simple
manger, a wooden trough to hold the hay
that animals ate. The second tree didn't
become the tall mast of an elegant ship, as it
had dreamed, but instead it became the sides
of an ordinary fishing boat like many others
on the Sea of Galilee. The third didn't
become part of a tall tower, as it had dreamed,
but was fashioned into the beams of a cross
and used for a crucifixion.*

Notes

Introduction

1. Henry Glassie, *Irish Folk Tales* (New York: Pantheon Books, 1985), p. 110.
2. Mystic, Conn.: Twenty-Third Publications.

I

1. Richard A Schoenherr and Annette Sorensen, *From the Second Vatican Council to the Second Millennium: Deadline and Change in the U.S. Catholic Church,* "Cross Respondent Report: 5, A Report of the Comparative Religious Organization Studies" (University of Wisconsin-Madison, 1981). Hereafter referred to as *Decline and Change.*
2. Letters to the Editor, *National Catholic Reporter,* 10 September 1985.
3. *Decline and Change,* pp. 23, 44-45.
4. *Lumen Gentium,* 32.
5. Joseph Cardinal Bernardin, *In Service of One Another: Pastoral Letter on Ministry* (The Chicago Catholic Publishing Company, 1985).
6. Reinhold Neibuhr, "From Life's Sidelines," *The Christian Century.*
7. *New York Times* (5 December 1985), page A12.

II

1. *Church,* Charter Issue, p. 44.
2. Joseph Gallagher, *The Pain and the Promise: Dairy of a City Priest* (New York: Doubleday, 1984), p. 84.
3. Archbishop Roger Mahoney, *Origins,* Vol. 15, No. 4 (19 September 1985), pp. 213-214.
4. *National Catholic Reporter* (22 November 1985), p. 21.
5. Joseph Krastel, C.SS.R., "Priests and the Need to be Needed," *The Priest* (April 1985), p. 4.

III

1. Robert Sherry, "Shortage? What Vocation Shortage?" *The Priest* (November 1985), p. 29 ff.

197

2. As quoted in *The Priest* (September 1985), p. 30.
3. William Barry, "Women and the Priesthood," *The Tablet* (26 October 1985), p. 121.
4. *Christianity and Crisis* (6 September 1985), p. 431.
5. John J. Begley and Carl J. Armbuster, *The American Ecclesiastical Review* (1971), p. 165.
6. Andrew M. Greeley, *American Catholics Since the Council: An Unauthorized Report* (Chicago: Thomas More Press), p. 120.
7. Dan Wakefield, "Returning to Church," *New York Times Magazine* (22 December 1985), pp. 17 ff.
8. John Tracy Ellis, *Origins*.
9. Timothy Sims, "Learning from the Fundamentalists," *The Christian Century* (11 December 1985), p. 1140.
10. Kenneth C. Haugk, "Lay Ministry: The Unfinished Reformation," *The Christian Ministry* (November 1985), p. 5.
11. William E. Hulme, Milo L. Brekke, and Willian C. Behrens, *Pastors in Ministry* (Minneapolis: Augsburg, 1985).
12. Daniel Flaherty, "No Pastor, No Building, No Debt," *Church* (Fall 1985), p. 20.
13. Dean R. Hoge, "For the Record: What Catholics Want From Their Priests," *Church* (Winter 1985), p. 46.
14. *U.S. Catholic* (December 1985), p.

IV

1. Andrew M. Greeley, *American Catholics*, p. 121.
2. *Origins*, Vol. 15, No. 21 (7 November), p. 359.
3. Robert Imbelli, "The Priest in America Today" in *Where We Are: American Catholics in the 1980s*, ed. Michael Glazier (Wilmington, Del.: Michael Glazier, 1985). Hereafter *Where We Are.*
4. John Heagle, *The Critic* (Winter 1985), pp. 88-89.
5. April and June 1985.
6. John E. Manzo, Letters to the Editor (6 November, 1985), p. 1013.
7. Andrew M. Greeley, *American Catholics*, p. 119.
8. Thomas J. Peters and Robert H. Waterman, Jr., *In Search of Excellence* (New York: Warner Books, 1984), p.58.
9. Peters and Waterman, pp. 239-40.
10. Arthur Jones in *The National Catholic Reporter* (19 July 1985).
11. See James J. Gill, S.J., M.D., "Why So Few Vocations?" *Human Development* (Spring 1986), p. 10.

V

1. Robert Imbelli, p. 122.
2. Peter Fink, "The Sacrament of Orders: Some Liturgical Reflections," *Worship*, Volume 56, No. 6 (November 1981), pp. 489-490.
3. Fink, pp. 491-492.
4. David N. Power, *Gifts That Differ: Lay Ministries Established and Unestablished* (New York: Pueblo, 1980), p. 127.

5. John H. Westerhoff III and William H. Willimon, *Liturgy and Learning: Through the Life Cycle* (New York: Seabury Press, 1980), p. 144.
6. Dom Gregory Dix, *The Shape of the Liturgy* (New York: Seabury Press, 1982), p. 12.
7. John Coleman, "A Theology of Ministry," *The Way*, Volume 25, No. 1 (January 1985), p. 8.
8. Quoted by John A. Coleman, "A Theology of Ministry," *The Way* (January 1985), p. 16.
9. *Origins* Volume 15, No. 18 (17 October 1985), p. 305.
10. "Leadership for Excellence," *Human Development* Vol. 6, No. 4 (Winter 1985), p. 8.
11. James Adams and Cecilia A. Hahn, "Learning to Share the Ministry" (Washington, DC: The Alban Institute, 1985), 57. 12. Dennis Campbell, "The Ordained Ministry as a Profession: Theological Reflections on Identity," *Quarterly Review* 3/2 (Summer 1983).

VI

1. *Commonweal* (12 July 1985), p. 400.
2. Anthony E. Gillis, *St. Anthony Messenger*.
3. *U.S. Catholic Historial*, Volume 4, No. 3 and 4 (1985) pp. 259-269.
4. The Alban Institute (May-June 1985), p. 2.
5. The Alban Institute, p. 3.

VII

1. Robert Lockwood, *Our Sunday Visitor* (3 October 1985), p. 131.
2. Ralph Mattson and Arthur Miller, *Finding a Job You Can Love* (Nashville: Thomas Nelson Press, 1982).
3. Jerry Foley, "Monday Morning Ministry," *Today's Parish* (October 1985) p. 25. Foley is currently working full time on how the church can best support the laity in their vocation.
4. Joe Holland, *PACE 15* (1984-1985), p. 1.
5. Jerry Foley, p. 25.
6. *Origins* Volume 15, No. 19 (24 October 1985) pp. 321-322.
7. Mary D. Attansio, *New York Times* (20 November 1985).
8. Reprinted by permission from GIFTS, published by the USCC Bishops' Committee on the Laity.
9. Allison Hahn, "Where in the World Is the Church?" *Christian Ministry* (November 1985), p. 9.
10. Michael Murphy, ed., "Old Thorns and Old Priests," *Christian Ministry* (November 1985), pp. 71-72.

VIII

1. Report No. 1 (December 1984).
2. See Jay Dolan, *The American Catholic Experience* (New York: Doubleday, 1985).
3. Action Information, The Alban Insitute.

4. Mentioned briefly in my book, *Ministry: Traditions, Tensions, and Transitions* (Mystic, Conn.: Twenty-Third Publications, 1982).
5. If you want not only the entire census but also a 134-page booklet of suggestions for, and ways to start, parish ministries, write to: St. Mary's Parish, Box H, Colts Neck NJ 07722.
6. Madeleine L'Engle, *The Sphinx at Dawn* (New York: Seabury Press, 1982).

IX

1. Bernard Swain, *Commonweal* (4 October 1985), p. 525.
2. Joan Puls, O.S.F., *Every Bush Is Burning* (Mystic, Conn.: Twenty-Third Publications, 1985), p. 5
3. John Carmody, *Wholistic Spirituality* (Mahwah, N.J.: Paulist Press, 1983), p. 135.
4. James Fenhagen, *Laity Exchange* (Andershaw Documents), p. 142.
5. Andrew M. Greeley.
6. Garrison Keillor, *Lake Wobegon Days* (New York: Viking Press, 1985), p. 2.
7. Margaret Miles, *Image As Insight* (Boston: Beacon Press, 1985), pp 102-03.
8. Thomas Merton, *The Seven Story Mountain* (Harcourt, Brace & Co., 1948), pp. 202-203.
9. *Ms.* (July 1985), pp. 43-44.
10. Robert Weiss, *Family Process* (March 1985).
11. James B. Nelson, SIECUS Report, Volume XIII, No. 4 (March 1985).

X

1. Used with permission. Appears in *Christian Short Stories,* ed. by Mark Booth (New York: Crossroad, 1984).

XI

1. Joseph Gallagher, *The Pain and the Privilege,* p. 25.
2. *Church* (January 1986), p. 42.
3. San Francisco: Harper & Row, 1978.
4. *U.S. Catholic* (December 1985), p. 28.
5. George B. Wilson, "Some Versions of 'Pastoral,' " *America* (10 November 1984), pp. 289 ff.

XII

1. Dorothy Sayers, *Gaudy Night* (new york: Avon Books, 1936), p.17.

XIII

1. Thomas Archdeacon, *New York Times Book Review,* p. 27.

XIV

1. The canonical source for the ideas of this chapter come from Father Griffin who is a canon lawyer and was present as an expert at the Bruges meeting. He gave a talk on his experience there and on canon law at the national meeting of diocesan planners in San Francisco in February 1986. A fine videotape entitled "New Ways of Being Church," which is an account of the Bruges meeting, may be obtained from Ecclesia Localis Documentation Center, 199 E. Thompson Ave, West St. Paul, MN 55118.

2. Philip J. Murnion, "The Community Called Parish," *Church* (Winter 1985), p. 8. His models of parish are not unlike mine in *Ministry: Traditions, Tensions, and Transitions* (Mystic, Conn.: Twenty-Third Publications, 1982).

Reverend William J. Bausch is a Roman Catholic priest who has written many books and spoken to numerous groups during the thirty years of his priesthood. But first and foremost, William Bausch is a pastor. For the people and community of St. Mary's in Colts Neck, New Jersey, he has been pastor for twenty years.

Throughout all his visionary work as an enabler of the laity, in the spirit of the Second Vatican Council, Father Bausch has never lost sight of the particularity of priesthood and the singular and pristine charism of the priest.

Now in *Take Heart, Father* a trilogy of books comes to fruition for Father Bausch. Now the priest and the pastor become the focus of care and concern, of development and growth. It is fitting that after two books for his parishioners and those beyond the parish who have shared in his vision of the parish (*The Christian Parish*, 1980) and ministry (*Ministry: Traditions, Tensions, Transitions*, 1984), Father Bausch now rounds out this vision with an equally sensitive, knowledgeable, and prophetic volume on priests and the priesthood.